The Elements of Human Nature

Using Behavioral Science to
Solve Problems in Life,
Business, & Policy

Ryan A. Kueter

CONTENTS

Preface   1

I   **MOTIVATION**   4
    The Private Interest Theory of Motivation   5
    Motivating Productivity   7
    Marketing & Persuasion   8
    Value Creation   10
    Why People Make Terrible Decisions   12

II **JUDGMENT**   14
    Habits   15
    Heuristics   16
    Biases   17
    Reducing Uncertainty   19
    Quality of Information   23
    Limitations on Judgment   25
    Diminishing Returns on Information   29
    Ethical Decisions & the Conscience   30

III **SATISFACTION**   33
    Life Satisfaction   34
    The Influence of Gains & Losses   39
    Economic Influences   42
    Political Influences   44

IV **PRODUCTIVITY**   47
    Vision & Creativity   48
    Strategy   49
    Opportunity Costs   50
    Risk Tolerance   52
    Risk Mitigation   53
    Commitment   55

V   **CONDITIONING**   57
    The Principle of Conditioning   58
    Changing the Brain   59
    Empirical Discovery   61
    Self-Confidence   62
    Agents of Encouragement   65
    Agents of Adversity   67
    Physical Conditioning   73

CONTENTS

VI   **RESPONSIBILITY**   76
The Meaning of Responsibility   76
Scope of Responsibility   78
Obligations   81
Answering for Decisions   83
Rationalization   85
Manipulation   87
Obstruction   88
Increasing Responsibility   90
Accountability   92
Problems of Accountability   93

VII   **STRESSORS**   95
Health Related Outcomes   96
Biological Influences   98
The Fear Response   100
Stress Response Habits   102

VIII   **MENTAL DISORDERS**   106
Relationships & Mental Health   107
Mental Disorders   109
The Cost of Mental Disorders   111
Depression   112
Schizophrenia   114
Substance Use Disorder   114
Recognizing a Mental Health Problem   117

IX   **SOCIAL SKILLS**   119
Strengthening Relationships   120
Dependability   120
Communication Skills   122
Conflict Resolution Skills   123
Ending Harmful Relationships   125

X   **SOCIAL RESPONSIBILITY**   127
Social Problems   128
Public Goods & Services   129
Influences on Policy   130
Approaches to Mitigating Social Problems   132
A Different Approach   137

REFERENCES   140
INDEX   147

PREFACE

The true value of Psychology does not simply come from making discoveries about behavior, or how the brain works. It comes from using those discoveries to solve challenging problems, like helping people to make better decisions, creating realistic solutions for reducing social problems, improving business operations, and understanding the impact of public policy.

To solve those problems, this book isolates ten universal elements of behavior that have the most influence on life outcomes. They include motivation, judgment, life satisfaction, productivity, conditioning, responsibility, stressors, mental disorders, social skills, and social responsibility. To study these elements, this book draws from a variety of different research methods, including naturalistic observation, case studies, experimental research, and history, for evidence to prove, or disprove, certain theories. At times, this book briefly looks at the relationship between biology and behavior. But it primarily focuses on observing how behaviors may be elicited, changed, or improved with practice to improve performance, or by developing them into a habit to make them more automatic, or by changing the environment to increase personal satisfaction.

Another challenging problem this book tackles is developing a useful and practical theory of motivation. Having a general theory of motivation is not only useful in Psychology, which seeks to explain the causes of human behavior, but in Economics, Marketing, and other subjects that already have working theories in practice. The first chapter introduces a unifying theory of motivation that applies across many fields of research and is used to explain many behaviors that would otherwise be unexplainable.

This book also devotes a chapter to exploring mental health, which is not common knowledge today like physical health. People may know how to improve their physical health with diet, exercise, and nutrition. And most people may know that, in terms of physical health, illness occurs as a result of a pathogen, like an infection from a virus or disease, or from poisoning. But people, today, may not know the attributes of mental health, or understand mental disorders and their role in mental health problems.

Several chapters in this book explore how people improve their overall mental and physical condition, not just by eating healthy or exercising, but by learning, improving judgment when making risky or impactful decisions, improving self-confidence, eliciting and strengthening different types of responses, and improving performance. Each of these has applications in relationships, parenting, management, and leadership. And each is a significant part of personal development that influences whether people develop into independent and responsible adults who have enough perceived control over life to solve the problems standing in the way of creating the futures they want.

Another challenge of Psychology involves creating programs aimed at mitigating social problems (i.e., problems that have a negative impact on people or society) by addressing some of the known causes of those problems. A chapter on conditioning, for example, explores how disorders, like Post Traumatic Stress Disorder (PTSD) and some emotional disorders, develop as a result of prolonged exposure to adverse conditions, and cause mental or behavioral problems that sometimes develop into social problems. Those disorders have environmental origins, rather than genetic origins, and may be preventable and treatable.

And, lastly, this book looks at the potential for using Behavioral Science to help political leaders make better decisions about public policy and programs. If policy makers, or their advisors, could collect sufficient data about the long-term social and economic consequences of a policy, in terms of how it impacts the lives of citizens and local economies, they could be more effective at creating policies that improve satisfaction among citizens.

CHAPTER I:
MOTIVATION

Whether a Psychologist is studying brain anatomy, neural networks, or the link between genes and behavior, that person is, in some way, studying why people behave the way they do. Or, in other words, that person is studying motivation. But developing a general unified theory of motivation has proven to be one of the more elusive and difficult problems of human psychology. This chapter introduces a theory of motivation that is applicable across a range of human sciences, and is used throughout this book to explain many different types of behavior.

The study of motivation has many real-world applications in leadership, education, and parenting. And subjects, like Economics, already use a theory of motivation to study economic behavior. A little knowledge about motivation is useful to managers who want to motivate workers to perform at a higher level, as we will see later in this chapter, or when trying persuade a hiring manager that you are the best candidate for a job. Marketing professionals and business owners must motivate people to buy their goods or services or they would eventually go out of business. And knowing how to motivate people is powerful, in a way, because it enables you to persuade people, to gain their help and support.

1
The Private Interest Theory of Motivation

If we view human behavior as a series of decisions consisting of actions, or inaction, then we could study behavior by looking at its influencing causes and outcomes. Decisions are influenced by a variety of biological and environmental motivators, some of which include social interaction, sexual hormones, stress hormones, diseases, aging, life experiences, and what we learn from those experiences. Behavior is profoundly influenced neurological conditions, sleepiness, chemistry, substance use, and mental disorders. A person may be less motivated, more stressed, and more inclined to make poorer decisions when certain areas of the brain, like the prefrontal cortex, do not perform well. And engaging in learning and physical activities may improve brain function, which could further improve judgment and a person's ability to make better, more deliberate, decisions.

All of these biological or environmental motivators shift our interests towards or away from wanting certain things. If we are tired or sleepy, we may want to take a nap on the couch. If we are hungry, we may be interested in what is in the cupboard. Or if we face the prospect of spending long hours in rush-hour traffic, we may start looking for an alternate route to our destination. All of these different motivators poke and prod us to move in many different directions, and shift our interests and what we attend to in the moment. The idea that these motivators influence what we want and, in doing so, influence our own private interests forms the basis of the Private Interest Theory of Motivation.

This theory follows a very basic tendency in human behavior: We tend to pick-up on, attend to, and want, things that spark our interest, and put down and abandon things that lose our interests. The more we are interested in something, the more we want to see it, have it, learn about it, or experience it. The more we want something, the more our interest, and passion for it, increases. We may even place monetary exchange value on something in the attempt to purchase it. Or we may protect and defend things we want to prevent losses. And the opposite may be true for things we lack interest in.

The idea that people are motivated by private interest shares some qualities with an Economic theory called the Rational Choice Theory, which views people as motivated by self-interest. The theory presumes that when people are behaving rationally, they make choices that are beneficial and lead to self-growth and advantage. This is used in Economic models to predict what types of choices a rational buyer or seller is likely to make in a given scenario, which is typically the optimal choice. But when applied to general Psychology, the Rational Choice Theory presents an egocentric and cynical view of human intentions that has some incongruities, starting with the fact that people are not always motivated to be self-serving.

People are not always inherently programmed to improve their lives, reach for rewards, avoid punishments, increase equity, selfishly look out for themselves, or protect themselves from death and destruction. They are sometimes motivated to behave irrationally and self-destructively, and make decisions that lead to unhappiness and dissatisfaction. People not only want the things they need to live, like basic necessities, sometimes they want things that are useless to their survival, or are plainly self-damaging. People may pursue interests that lead to personal happiness. But they also pursue interests that lead to misery and their ultimate demise. And, in later chapters, we look at some reasons why people are motivated to behave irrationally, some of which involve stress, mental disorders, or abusive relationships.

The ability to interpret the motives of other people is, by itself, a basic social skill that usually develops at a very early age. People who are unable to do that tend to misinterpret other people's behavior, and read too much into it. For example, suppose Jack borrows Bob's hedge clippers and promises to return them the next day. A week passes and Bob wants his clippers back. He begins to suspect that Jack is a selfish, uncaring SOB, who stole his hedge clippers. Should Bob be angry? In reality, Jack may actually be a very empathetic and caring person who simply forgot to return Bob's clippers. Maybe Jack was too busy volunteering at the local Mission, or pursuing other altruistic and selfless interests. A person who is unable to interpret the intentions and motivations of other people may start unnecessary conflicts, or have other misunderstandings.

2
Motivating Productivity

In Daniel Pink's book *Drive: The Surprising Truth About What Motivates Us*, he makes the case that people are more motivated by intrinsic rewards, rather than extrinsic rewards and punishments, like money or the threat of imprisonment suggested by the Rational Choice Theory.[57] He goes on to say that people do not always have to be compensated to perform work. The reason some Open Source projects are successful is not because people prefer to slavishly work for free, but because they have some intrinsic value to gain from it. Volunteers may enjoy donating their time and labor for free because they are engaging in an interesting activity, developing their skills, and gaining valuable experience. This intrinsic motivation, he says, has contributed to the rise of Wikipedia and the decline of traditional for-profit encyclopedias.

Pink cites a number of studies to show how increasing incentives, like monetary compensation, does not always increase the quality or quantity of work performed. And in some instances, the quality and quantity of work actually decreases, like when people take shortcuts to achieve goals, or when they are corrupted by the anticipation of increasing rewards. People also learn to perform work only when a reward is provided. If a parent pays a child to perform a chore, like taking out the garbage, that child may stop performing the chore in the absence of compensation. And despite the fact that people are often motivated by rewards and punishments, he argues, they are motivated by much more than the incentives proposed by conventional economic theories.

This intrinsic motivation that Pink writes about is unmistakably the pursuit of private interest. Passion often drives productivity and quality. But without interest, passion does not exist. This is why so many fully capable students fail in school. The extrinsic motivators of grades or scholarship are not enough to make them interested in the curriculum. If they were interested, they would voluntarily do it without being told, just like a person who enjoys a morning jog, or is genuinely intrigued about revealing the mysteries of human history, or is fascinated by the new capabilities they could discover while playing with robotics. An instructor may be able to spark a student's interests in a subject, not just by making it fun, but by showing the student what could be gained by learning about it, or what could be lost otherwise. Even the simple act of thinking, or talking, about an activity can stimulate interest and motivate a person to engage in the activity. But people are not motivated to do just anything for money. It must be within their frame of interest.

3
Marketing & Persuasion

Marketers primarily work by trying to attract the interests of potential buyers. Marketers do that by showing people what they gain by purchasing a product, how it entertains, improves their health, or makes them smarter or more attractive. They often use a tactic called emotional branding where they show an advertisement featuring people using the product while having fun, laughing, and entertaining. Advertisements that produce an emotional response in the audience, not only attract attention and interest to a product, they increase the desire to have the product.

Ultimately, the goal of marking is to influence buyer expectations about a good or service, to increase the urge to have it. Some of that anticipation may be influenced by what a person is told, or what a person experienced in the past. A person may invest in one's education, for example, because of what that person expects to gain in return. Those expectations may influence productivity, work ethic, behavior, and personal sacrifices. That person may spend a large sum of money to attend a four year university, or will study for months to earn a difficult industry certification, expecting to increase expertise or income.

Expectations influence buying behaviors in other ways. If a friend tells you that a Restaurant's food is terrible, maybe their sweat tea is really sour tea and their food could give you food poisoning, would you eat there? If a reporter wrote a scathing review about a product and said that he hates the product and would never use it, would it influence your decision to buy one? Or if you watched a car commercial and the actor in the commercial said that she was so happy and excited with the car, its warranty, and how it drives, would it persuade you to buy one? All of these are attempts to emotionally brand specific products, and primarily to influence buyer expectations and increase buyer interests in those things.

Our expectations are not only influenced by the marketing environment in which we live, but by past experiences, what we want, what we read, and what we imagine. If an advertisement convinces you that you could get rich quickly by handing someone a large sum of money for advice, you may do it. But you should also consider that your expectations are being influenced by the interests of other people. And you risk playing into their interests rather than making decisions that are best for you. If you see an ad that says "Live longer: Eat pistachios!," you may buy pistachios believing that eating pistachios will increase your longevity, when the advertiser really just wants you to buy pistachios. And consumers willingly spend money on those things, even if the claim is untrue, because the purchase is a low risk decision, and any potential losses are small and negligible. Besides, eating pistachios can be a healthy treat, whether it leads to a longer life or not.

4
Value Creation

Private interest leads to demand and value creation. The more a person wants something, the more that person may be willing to work and sacrifice for it, and place monetary exchange value on it. If you know what people like, and what they want, you can create demand. And if you are able to satisfy that demand, you can create value.

Demand for a good or service is largely shaped by a perception of how much people want something or, in other words, how strong their urge is to have it. In marketing, the whole purpose of advertisement is to divert a person's attention away from what they are doing to show them why they want a product. A marketing team may try to make a viral advertisement that is so interesting, entertaining, or unbelievable that it is redistributed and shared among a target demographic. And that attracts more attention to the brand or the product they are selling. The ability to control attention and awareness when marketing a product is powerful because it attracts interest, influences behavior, and changes people's buying habits.

To motivate a person to do anything, you have to generate interest and create the urge to do it. A product needs to be good enough for people to like it and want it. In the food industry, people consume because the food satisfies their hunger, or because it is delicious. These are qualities that add value, and increase the amount that people want, and are willing to pay for, an item. Business managers and product developers are financially incentivized to innovate, change, and improve their products, to make them more appealing than other competitive offerings. In each of these scenarios, people are trying to increase other people's want for something, to attract interest and create value.

Private interest not only creates monetary value, it creates personal and cultural value and shapes people's likes and dislikes, along with their opinions, beliefs, and consumption habits. A college of mine who is a father of three girls collected science fiction memorabilia, posters, and small figurines. He would spend a considerable amount of time searching for an item he was interested in, shaking boxes, and buying entire displays of small plastic figurines. He once told me about a time when he bought an entire display and returned to the store the next day to see if they had more. A store employee told him they were sold-out because some guy bought the entire display the previous day. A significant portion of his annual earnings would go to buying those things, not for his girls, but for himself. When I mentioned this to an acquaintance, he said he would never waste even the smallest amount of money on those things, especially not for himself.

People value things differently depending on their unique interests. A wealthy person may be interested in buying a million dollar piece of artwork for many different reasons. Maybe the person is interested appealing to a certain class of people, wants to make a statement about personal values, wants to possess something that is rare, or wants the best that the world has to offer. Or maybe the art is an investment, a way of diversifying one's portfolio by putting money into a security that may appreciate in value. But from the least expensive things to the most expensive things, the more a person wants something, the more that person may be willing to sacrifice, in terms of time, money, and labor to obtain it.

5
Why People Make Terrible Decisions

People, whether they are private citizens or national leaders, make terrible decisions for many reasons. Behavior is heavily influenced by what we attend to in the moment. We are inclined to respond to immediate conditions, like hunger, emotions, tiredness, or the loud noise we just heard. People are naturally excitable and sometimes allow instinct, like emotions and fears, to dictate their actions rather than deliberate reason. And those things often drive our interests and behavior, more so than distant future outcomes.

These distractions are one reason people often fail when trying to achieve longer-term goals. The circumstances they are confronted with, and their emotions in the moment, dominate their attention and direct their actions. What we want in the moment distracts us from what we ultimately want in our future. And despite our ability to think strategically and consider longer-term consequences, we spend more of our time attending to immediate interests, and are frequently drawn away from our longer-term goals, sometimes to the point of acting against our best interests.

Consider why a woman would commit a marital infidelity in a marriage where the husband would divorce her if he discovers the infidelity. Maybe she was enraptured by overwhelming and uncontrollable sexual excitement as she was seduced by an irresistibly attractive man who tempted her to engage in an experience that is, for her, more a fantasy than reality. The choice she made may not be a life goal, but it became an immediate sexual interest that clouded her longer-term vision.

People who exhibit obsessive interests, or have addictions to certain pleasures, like gambling or drugs, may experience similar episodes. Most people are able to gamble, or have a drink, and do not lose control over their desire for those things. But people who begin to anticipate the reward from the experience and frequently engage in those activities are more at risk of addiction. Engaging in the behavior with increasing frequency only further exposes the addict to other unwanted risks associated with the behavior, like the unwanted behavioral and financial consequences, legal problems, and side-effects created by the addiction.

So part of the reason people sometimes make terrible decisions has to do with their motivation and interests in any given moment. Adam may want to learn a new language, but complains that he does not have time because he is too busy laying on the couch and watching television. Or maybe he spends too much money on something that is unnecessary while paying down a debt. Or he overindulges in a three course meal while on a weight-loss program. He gives in to his wants and urges in the moment, and loses focus on his longer-term goals.

CHAPTER II:
JUDGMENT

In the first chapter, we looked at how behavior is a series of decisions consisting of actions, or inaction. And those decisions are influenced by motivators, like hormones, chemistry, social influences, among many other factors. When responding to those motivators, we use our judgment to consider which opportunities are best for us from the limited choices. And that judgment goes into making the final decision.

Judgment is influenced by many factors, depending on the outcomes we are trying to create. If we are engineering a piece of machinery, judgment may be influenced by mathematical precision. If we were writing a persuasive speech, creating a piece of artwork, or writing a song, our judgment may be influenced by the ability to convey an emotion. But when making a decision that is risky, or impacts people's lives, our judgment may be influenced by other factors, like habits, intuition, and biases, that lead to mistakes and errors in thinking. And in this chapter, we look at those factors in addition to some ways to improve judgment when making risky and impactful decisions.

1
Habits

Many decisions are made by habit (i.e., a learned response to routine circumstances) that become more automatic with repetition. Habits influence how we interact with people, do business, stay productive, study and learn, spend time and money, and entertain. People develop habits for personal safety, like locking doors, buckling seatbelts, or wearing safety gear. People develop habits for socializing, by introducing themselves, and being polite. And people develop buying habits, in terms of the items they purchase regularly. Habits change as people get married, have children, or get a divorce. Some habits improve health, like eating nutritious food, while others do harm, like drinking excessive amounts of alcohol.

In the *Power of Habit: Why We Do What We Do in Life and Business*, New York Times journalist Charles Duhigg explores the science and applications of habits in a variety of different subjects including neurology, business, marketing, and sports. In the first chapter, he talks about the structure of a habit, as identified by MIT researchers, and how habits are triggered by cues.[24] Deciding to eat lunch because it's noon time or deciding to wash hands because they are dirty, are habits triggered by environmental cues. And habits differ by complexity. But the one thing they all have in common is that the amount of mental effort required to perform them decreases as they are repeated and learned, so that performing habituated tasks becomes easier and more automatic with time.

Habits are partially fixed and predictable as they become more automatic. And they are partially malleable and changeable as new habits form. Ideally, if you want to change what you eat, how you work, or how you approach other people, you need to develop new habits, and learn new ways of responding to those routine circumstances.

Parents may be able to influence a child's habits by discouraging unwanted behaviors, or by encouraging wanted behaviors. Management is able to change the way an organization operates by changing the habits of workers, by providing training and developing customer service and communication skills.

But the problem with developing new habits is that human behavior tends to follow the path of least resistance and defaults back to responses that require the least amount of effort, thought, and uncertainty. Engaging in a well established pattern behavior is easier and presents more certainty than engaging in a new and unfamiliar behavior that requires more thinking and effort, and may lead to an unsatisfactory outcome. Since old stimulus-responses are already conveniently hard-wired into the brain, learned, and automatic, they require very little effort. But, as we will see in a later chapter on conditioning, it is possible to learn new behaviors and strengthening specific responses with repetition.

2

Heuristics

The term heuristic was originally developed by Psychologists Amos Tversky and Daniel Kahneman to describe a rule of thumb, or some intuitive technique, for making decisions when faced with uncertainty. Using heuristics, and making decisions based on intuition, is our default mode of thinking as we respond to everyday circumstances. The majority of outcomes we are trying to create, and the goals we seek to achieve, are often easily obtainable, like cleaning our living space. These are small and manageable tasks that do not require much mental effort to complete. Making decisions about what vegetables are good to eat only require a little common sense by seeing, smelling, and tasting a vegetable to know that it is good to eat, rather than researching how long a vegetable lasts or consulting with an expert. We only need a small amount of information gleaned from our senses and intuition to avoid making a mistake in most daily circumstances.

But when we make decisions based on intuition, we do not always have sufficient information to be certain about the outcomes we are creating. People tend to ignore a substantial amount of information and are inclined to make decisions based on guesses, probability, emotions, and beliefs. People are compelled to explain things, or accept something as true, despite the fact that they do not have enough evidence to support their conclusions. Habitually relying on heuristics may be enough to get us through the day. But when making decisions that are risky, or impact people's lives or the future of organizations, it can have terrible and life-altering consequences. Later in this chapter, we look at ways of reducing those mistakes.

3
Biases

Intuitive judgments inevitably lead to biases. Anytime a person uses intuition to choose "Item A" over "Item B" that person has created a reason to favor "Item A" over "Item B." In other words, that person has a bias. The most trivial and irrelevant details, like price, a person's opinion, an emotional response, or labeling, may cause a person to form a bias for or against something, whether the reasons for that bias are true or not. Some biases are more impactful than others. Favoring one type of food over another is a bias that has a very low impact on people. But biases that rob people of opportunity, like racial or ethnic discrimination, or cause serious injuries or death, tend to cause harm or loss, and create discontent.

Even the most superficial appearances bias the way a person is judged, according to Psychologist Alexander Todorov, who conducted a study to show that people tend to judge the competence of candidates in political elections based on their intuitive judgment of facial features, rather than the candidate's actual qualifications or capabilities. In his study, he asked participants to compare the portraits of candidates seeking election in the House or Senate and to judge their competence. The participants predicted the election's outcome more than 70% of the time, suggesting that facial features tend to bias voter's judgment of candidates. This type of bias, he suggested, may also influence hiring or promotion decisions.[42]

Recruiters and hiring managers, like all other people, make intuitive judgments and may have cognitive biases when seeking candidates for employment. They may have expectations about what the ideal candidate looks like, or acts like, or what kind of experience the person has, and may give preferential treatment to someone who exhibits those qualities, despite the candidate's actual qualifications. A candidate seeking employment may over-emphasize qualities, like gray hair, suit and tie, and charm, to give an impression. And that impression may influence a hiring manager's confidence in the person more than actual facts, like actual work experience, academic performance, qualifications, and proven successes.

Biases also influence people's beliefs about their own abilities, and their beliefs about other people. If you believe you are able to do something and someone else disagrees, your biased viewpoint may compel you to do it. Maybe you believe that you have an advantage on your side. An athlete may believe that a lucky rabbit's foot will help him, or his team, win a game. B. F. Skinner called these beliefs non-contingent reinforcement, which is a belief in the existence of a relationship between a behavior and its consequences, even when no such relationship exists.[63] In a similar way, religion provides something that science cannot easily replace: A belief in a greater power from which to draw strength and reassurance during difficult times. In the movie Star Wars, Obi-Wan Kenobi tells Luke Skywalker "may the force be with you" as he battles his nemesis Darth Vader. And, in the end, he draws strength from "The Force" to win the battle.

But overconfidence in certain abilities also leads to poor judgment and terrible decisions. A man may biasly believe that he has greater abilities than he does, or may deceive himself into believing that luck, or some advantage, is on his side. A gambler, for instance, may not know the outcome of a bet. But he, at least, knows he must gamble to win. This remains true, even when he continues losing all of his money while being optimistic that he will eventually succeed. Psychologists call this bias the Gambler's Fallacy, when people think that future probabilities are altered by past events. For example, if a coin-flip lands on heads five times in a row, a person may predict that the next flip will land on tails, despite the fact that the probability remains unchanged.[39]

4

Reducing Uncertainty

If people were omnipotent and knew everything, they could predict the outcome of any decision. But since that supernatural power is beyond human ability, we tend to make decisions based on intuition, which requires very little mental effort. In Daniel Kahneman's book *Thinking Fast and Slow*, he points out that thinking and calculating is labor intensive, inconvenient, and requires mental effort and the expenditure of energy.[40] People tend to expend the least amount of energy and effort necessary to make decisions. So they make decisions based on intuition and what is already present in their mind and senses.

The problem with using intuition is that it leads to mistakes. When people make low-risk, low-impact, decisions, like deciding what to eat for lunch, those mistakes are easily ignored and forgotten. But when decisions are risky, dangerous, or impact people's lives, like investing millions of dollars in a business venture without any prior knowledge, or doing something that causes people to experience significant losses, those decisions could have devastating consequences.

Uncertainty in decisions presents a risk of loss. And since intuition does not always provide enough information to be certain about potential outcomes, people are able to mitigate the risk of loss by seeking more information. Consider a doctor diagnosing an abnormal behavioral condition, like depression. If the doctor is inclined to believe that the condition has genetic origins without conducting a genetic test, or without considering all of the known causes, the doctor is more likely to make an incorrect diagnosis. In that circumstance, medication may treat the symptom, but may do nothing to treat the actual cause. The medication, then, may medicate the symptoms while the patient is working toward a permanent solution.

Ideally we would always make an informed decision. But the extent to which our decisions are truly informed is not always certain. We could smell a vegetable to make sure it's not spoiled. But we cannot always detect if water is contaminated with unsafe levels of lead or arsenic. And while you may have no reason to fear your drinking water, people underestimate how oblivious they are about the world they live in. They may continue drinking contaminated water believing it is just fine and ignore any evidence that suggests otherwise. Psychologists call the tendency to believe that choices are more informed than they really are a choice-supportive bias.

The chapters in this book present many different strategies for reducing uncertainty when making decisions, by seeking more information, consulting with an expert, or by experimenting and testing theories to see if they contain truth. In the book *Thinking Fast and Slow*, Kahneman points out that this concept also applies to statistics and collecting adequate sample sizes when conducting studies. He argues that a study on the cancer rate in rural areas with low populations would cause some researchers to conclude that a high incidence of cancer is attributed to the unhealthy and dirty rural lifestyle, or a low incidence of cancer is attributable to the healthy and clean rural lifestyle. Low sample sizes produce dramatically different results. And people see patterns, and attribute causes, to random events. But large sample sizes reduce uncertainty about a conclusion by providing enough data to reveal a more meaningful trend.[41]

Our ability to reduce uncertainty when making decisions depends partly on what we know, and partly on the effort we are willing to put into knowing more. People can learn a lot from experience, but only if they put in the effort to learn from that experience. Some of that learning process may involve trial and error, testing the validity of ideas, asking questions, and learning from mistakes. But unless you are an expert, or a seasoned professional, then your knowledge about a subject is limited. And the advice and information you receive from other people, even when they claim to know, is limited and uncertain and may be influenced by their own interests and beliefs.

When people gullibly and unwittingly believe whatever they are told, they are more likely to be taken advantage of. Instead of doing that, when using your own judgment, you could recognize and ignore things you do not know that are not worth your time or effort. Or you could do a little work, consider additional possibilities, and seek more information, to improve certainty in your final decision. Doing that not only reduces uncertainty and the likelihood of mistakes, it improves your judgment and dependability as a decision maker.

In the last chapter, we looked at why people make terrible decisions. Behavior tends to be influenced by what they attend to in the moment. People are inclined to respond to hunger, emotions, tiredness, or fear, and allow instinct, rather than deliberate reason, to dictate their actions. When people act on instinct, intuition, or fear, they have fewer reasons for making a decision, which may lead to irrational and sometimes terrible decisions, especially when they go horribly wrong. Seeking more information and considering more possibilities makes you a more rational decision maker because you have more information, more evidence, more possibilities, and more reasons for making a decision. The only problem with doing that is that it requires more work, like reading the terms of a contract before signing, or researching an expensive item before making a purchase. Even then, you may not have enough information to completely avoid mistakes, and may not be satisfied with the final result.

To illustrate this basic problem solving skill, imagine that Greg is a Technical Support Representative who works for a large computer manufacturer. A customer calls Tech Support with a problem. Sometimes the computer generates an error that indicates the cause of the problem. Other times, Greg is uncertain and needs to troubleshoot by testing suspect components to see which one is faulty. Greg's uncertainty about the cause of the problem does not always win the confidence of customers immediately. But if he is too overconfident, he may replace the wrong part. So through the process of elimination, starting with the most likely cause and the least destructive form of troubleshooting, Greg is able to solve the problem quickly. And customers are always satisfied with the resolution and fully confident in Greg's technical ability by the end of the call.

Solving problems in our daily lives is similar. Sometimes people worry too much about how they are judged and feel pressured to claim they have knowledge they do not. Consequently, they have errors in judgment, make mistakes, create problems, and lead themselves and other people in the wrong direction. By recognizing and reducing uncertainty, testing ideas, asking questions, doing research, and getting feedback, people are able to reduce mistakes and failure, and create more satisfying outcomes. Or to put it differently, people improve their chances of being correct when they are able to recognize what they do not know, and work to get the facts they need to know what they are talking about. The ability to suspend judgment until all of the evidence is considered helps to avoid wrong conclusions. This not only applies to solving difficult technical problems, or to doctors diagnosing complex illnesses, it applies to people solving everyday problems, whether they are drivers on the road, people reading news on the internet, a manager of a large organization, or a policy maker drafting a new law.

Abraham Maslow once wrote that "sufficient knowledge" enables people to solve problems and helps them in their moral and ethical choices when deciding their next course of action. As people become more knowledgeable, their choices and solutions become easier and more automatic. Knowledge, he said, "brings certainty of decision, action, choice and what to do." Even in opening the abdomen, the surgeon knows to remove the inflamed appendix before it bursts and kills the patient. This, he says, is "an example of truth dictating what must be done."[48] The result of having sufficient knowledge, or sufficient problem solving skills, is that people are able to proceed with life confidently because they know what to do, or are able to figure out our next course of action.

5
Quality of Information

Quality of information refers to the accuracy and value of information. People are able to have greater certainty in creating a specific outcome when they make decisions based on information that is true and accurate. For example, if you ask someone for directions, and you are given the wrong directions, you will probably not get to your destination any faster by following those directions.

This is why business managers try to make data driven decisions based on facts, rather than intuition or opinions, to avoid costly mistakes. If you do not know how much material to buy in the production of a good, you may end up with left over material that will go to waste, or you may not have enough material to produce enough goods to remain profitable. If a manager does not factor in his regular expenses, in terms of land, labor, and production costs, then he may be operating at a loss and not know it. If a store owner has shelves full of goods that never sell, then he loses the opportunity to make a profit on merchandise that could be sitting on those shelves.

Another problem with making decisions based on intuition, is that the quality of that information tends to be degraded by emotions, opinions, beliefs, and memory loss. A memory may be especially prone to errors in recollection, depending on how much it is tested for accuracy. But simply because we are told something, read something, or observe something, does not mean our conclusions about those things are entirely true or accurate.

Biases also degrade the quality of information. People ignore and filter out a considerable amount of information that does not support their beliefs, or help them obtain the things they want. Instead they often seek evidence that confirms their beliefs, a tendency Psychologists call a confirmation bias, or the expectancy effect. People who have a confirmation bias may completely ignore information that invalidates their belief, even when the belief is obviously untrue.

During the 1960's, Robert Rosenthal created an experiment to find evidence for this type of self-fulfilling prophecy, called the Pygmalion effect. The experiment divided up two groups of students. One group was assigned rats labeled as bright, and the other group was assigned rats labeled as dull. All of the rats originated from the same group and were believed to have the same level of intelligence. But, for some reason, students training the bright rats reported better results than the students with the dull rats.[34]

24

Quality of information tends to be degraded by what people are told. And despite popular belief, people who are infallible, never make mistakes, and never lie, simply do not exist. Even the most honest and credible people make exaggerated comments and have problems remembering every once in a while. And people accept unproven scientific theories as truth even when the evidence is scarce, misattributed, or inconclusive. People are motivated believe things, and recall events in ways, that serve their own interests. That fact does not mean that you should disbelieve or ignore those people. But you should use your own judgment, and seek the information you need, when deciding what is best for you.

Inevitably, this problem harkens back to the deep philosophical Socratic question: What is the truth? Is the truth something you see with your own eyes (e.g., I'll believe it when I see it)? Or is the truth a fact that exists in a book? A Scientist may say that the truth may be discovered using empirical techniques, using a systematic process of testing, collecting evidence, and validation, and ideally in a controlled environment. Researchers call this type of research primary research. But we obviously cannot conduct an experiment every time we want to know the truth about something. So we rely on information from other, secondary, sources. We rely on a reputable subject matter expert, or a widely accepted authority, who has already done much of that work for us. And by using that secondary source, we are able to collect evidence, test and validate our own knowledge, and improve the quality of the information our decisions are based on.

6

Limitations on Judgment

We have already seen how people improve their judgment by suspending their judgment until they have enough evidence to be certain about their decision. This is especially true when making critical decisions that could lead to costly mistakes and failures, and could significantly impact a business, community, or people's lives. In recent years, businesses have relied more on information systems that store vast amounts of data to analyze and compile reports and develop strategies that mitigate the unintended consequences of costly decisions. That data may also be used by Statisticians to collect sufficient sample sizes to reduce the margin of error. And while those systems may improve decisions; they are never fully capable of predicting what will happen. No matter how much information we have, or how accurate the information is, our decisions always involve uncertainty and risk.

In our private lives, doing the work necessary to make the optimal choice in every set of circumstances has a significant cost because it consumes time and energy, and prevents us from responding to fleeting opportunities. Most of the outcomes we pursue in our daily lives are small, manageable, and make marginal improvements, like being productive, being creative, exploring the world, engaging in an enjoyable activity, and adapting to new situations. Intuition is better suited for those types of low-risk, low-impact, decisions, because a little trial and error, and learning from mistakes, is necessary to learn and make progress. Questioning whether we are informed enough to proceed confidently is not always the best strategy when solving the minor problems in the way of achieving life goals.

Even when people have more choices, and better opportunities, they sometimes experience a lapse in judgment and make terrible decisions. In the book *Nudge: Improving Decisions About Health, Wealth, and Happiness*, Richard Thaler and Cass Sunstein make the case that it may be possible to help people make better choices by creating choice architectures, which are ways of arranging the environment to influence people's choices. An example of a choice architecture would be how a manager arranges a Supermarket by putting certain items in checkout lanes to influence buyer decisions. Those items tend to be things that people forget, or buy on impulse, like batteries, novelty items, or candy that provokes child nagging.

Thaler and Sunstein suggest that choice architectures may also be used to help people make choices that are in their long-term interests. They argue that people tend to be loss averse and are motivated more by the fear of losses than they are by the prospect of gains. Spending money on health insurance or a retirement savings account are some examples. Younger adults have little motivation to put the small amount of money they earn in a retirement fund. So Thaler and Sunstein suggest that employers could provide a default option, which would automatically enroll employees in a retirement fund. Employees would, then, be allowed to opt out, if they choose to.[65]

While adding default options to contractual agreements, business processes, and the technologies we use, makes life easier, and may improve specific outcomes; it has significant limitations. Default options cannot be added to every choice we make. Thaler and Sunstein acknowledged that much and added that people are sometimes nudged into decisions that are not in their best interests and are, instead, in the interests of other people. Businesses are notorious for creating default options that play into their profit margins rather than the interests of paying customers by making false promises, or by taking advantage of unsuspecting buyers.

Charles Duhigg suggested another way of helping people to make smarter choices in his book *Smarter Faster Better: The Secrets of Being Productive in Life and Business*, by simplifying and reducing large amounts of information into a few simple choices.[25] A ten page insurance plan, or seven page wine menu, is overwhelming to a person who is not an expert. All of that information must be processed and researched to reduce uncertainty when trying to make the most satisfying choice. And the overwhelming nature of the task may force the buyer to either make a random choice, which may be a terrible decision, or give-up and make no choice at all. Simplifying large amounts of information into a few simple choices makes those choices easier and more intuitive.

Consulting with a subject matter expert who has already done that work for us is another way of simplifying the process. When trying to select the right wine, we could ask a Wine Connoisseur to provide advice about the different wines, their sweetness, the foods they complement, and the best vintages to help us make the best choice. Or we could download one of dozens of wine apps to our mobile device, which may help to reduce uncertainty about which wine to choose, assuming it is unbiased and not sponsored by a wine producer who is trying to promote their brand of wine.

Software is gradually making complex decisions more manageable by simplifying information and making complex data sets simple and intuitive. Corporate executives often rely on Business Intelligence software to provide a dashboard that displays simple charts to illustrate and summarize production, expenses, revenues, and other factors of operation, to make what would otherwise be difficult and complex business decisions, more intuitive.

Similarly, the primary job of project managers, in some organizations, is to work with subject matter experts to breakup complex tasks into simpler, more manageable tasks, to get a realistic estimate of the costs and the time necessary to create a manageable plan for project completion. The ability to simplify complex problems into simple intuitive choices, not only reduces errors in calculating estimates in budgets and project timelines, it reduces serious errors in judgment that could potentially bankrupt a business. The only downside is that doing so usually requires a significant amount of problem solving, labor, and work.

Whether choices are made simple for us or we must do a little work to figure out the best choice, we are the primary decision makers concerning our future. And we cannot always depend on someone else, like a personal advisor, government agency, or technology, to solve our unique problems or save us from our poor choices. People need to learn how to use their own judgment to solve problems unique to their own lives, and recognize and reduce uncertainty in their decisions to create outcomes they will be satisfied with.

7

Diminishing Returns on Information

Diminishing returns, in Economics, refers to the idea that as the amount of an input in the production of a good increases, holding all other inputs constant, the output also increases. But at some point, no matter how much of that input we add, the amount of output begins to diminish. This principle also applies to information when reducing uncertainty. People only need sufficient information to make the most satisfactory choice.

When we initially begin to collect information about a decision, the choice we make may change from one extreme to another depending on what we learn. To illustrate this idea, imagine Margaret is moving to a new city and is trying to make a decision about which of two neighborhoods she wants to move into: Towering Oaks or Winding Trails. She really wants to live in a safe neighborhood that is close to her child's school. And the housing in Towering Oaks is considerably less expensive and closer to a school. So her choice looks like it is going to be easy. But after doing a little research, she discovers that Towering Oaks has one of the highest crime rates in the city and that Winding Trails is one of the safest.

Since we always risk not having enough information, we could always mitigate that risk by seeking more information. But at some point, we have enough information to make our decision, and any additional information does not change our decision or its outcome.

8
Ethical Decisions & the Conscience

Our conscience (i.e., our ability to distinguish between right and wrong) is strongly influenced by judgment when making decisions, especially when those decisions impact other people's lives. Part of the problem is that, by default, people think intuitively. They attach emotions and labels to things as a shortcut when making decisions. If someone tells a horrible story about a person or place, it may influence the audience's perception of risk and how they interact with those things. And people can be very malicious and destructive toward innocent people, even when they do not have malicious intent.

A person who was wrongfully convicted of a crime is an example. In the past, when a police officer was convinced of a suspect's guilt, the officer may have used interrogation techniques that involved threat or coercion to get the suspect to confess. Officers who had a confirmation bias may have sought evidence that confirmed their suspicion rather than evidence that contradicted it. They would tell suspects that evidence already points to their guilt. And if they confessed, they would receive a lesser sentence, or would avoid the death penalty. And suspects who did not understand the legal process willingly complied, especially if they were children, had a mental disability, were mentally impaired by drugs or alcohol, or were subjected to an exhausting interrogation and were told that if they confessed, they could prove their innocence at a later time.[38]

To prevent these types of false confessions, the United Kingdom passed the Police and Criminal Evidence Act (PACE) in 1984, and created a police interrogation training program called PEACE. Before the training, officers who were unskilled interviewers may have presumed the suspect's guilt and only listened to the incriminating parts of the interview to build a strong case and get a charge. But officers who follow the law are prohibited from lying to suspects and are trained to collect reliable information based on the suspect's account. Following these guidelines should help to reduce the likelihood of false confessions and keep society safe by actually convicting perpetrators of crimes, rather than innocent people.[33]

News, and online media, also influence people's opinions. And since the Internet has become an influential source of information, the need for better media literacy has grown, in addition to helping people use better judgment when posting online or reading online news. Some businesses that profit from reporting the news may be incentivized to sell more news by reporting shocking allegations, whether those allegations are true or not. Online fake news, or satire news, makes click-revenue from advertisements by reporting unbelievable or shocking stories. Research scientists sometimes use a similar tactics when making exaggerated claims about the progress they are making to attract more funding. The more incredible the claims are, the more attention they receive and the more money they make.

Reporters who write the news may also be politically or criminally biased, and may tell only one side of a story. And that biased journalism may lead the audience to believe something that is not true, like believing that all abnormal behavioral conditions are the result of genes, despite the fact that some conditions are known to be caused by traumatic experiences. Or an innocent person may be convicted and imprisoned for committing a crime, or a guilty person may be set free, if not by a court of law, then by the court of public opinion.

Because people tend to think intuitively, they sometimes make judgments and form conclusions that are not only wrong, in the sense that they are mistaken and incorrect, but are morally wrong because of the senseless damage and hardship it causes. A direct relationship exists between being correct or incorrect, and righteous and wrong-ful behavior. And not knowing how to recognize uncertainty and suspend judgment may unintentionally lead to very immoral, cold-hearted, and callous actions.

CHAPTER III:
SATISFACTION

Personal satisfaction has a profound influence on human behavior, influencing a person's emotional state, productivity, and life goals. Satisfaction, or dissatisfaction, may be expressed, and objectively observed, in many different forms. Happiness may indicate satisfaction, and sadness or anger may indicate dissatisfaction. Emotional states, like happiness, sadness, or anger, are temporary and are indicators of personal satisfaction. Ongoing sources of dissatisfaction may repeatedly evoke emotions, like anger, that could develop into pattern behaviors and strengthen, and influence how people approach circumstances, as well as their self-confidence, overall attitude, and outlook on life.

But dissatisfaction is also a motivating force when it compels people to be productive and solve problems. When people are dissatisfied with something in their lives, instead of getting emotional about it, they may try to change it. People are willing to delay gratification, risk experiencing pain or loss, and sacrifice their time, energy, and enjoyment of life to have something that will bring them greater satisfaction. If you are not satisfied with the interi-

or design of your living space, you may continue to work on it, rethink it, and redesign it, until you are fully satisfied. The same could be said about learning, social life, or any other life goal.

People are not only motivated to be productive to create a more satisfying life for themselves, they have an incentive to provide a satisfactory performance in their life roles. If an employee continues to miss work regularly, the manager of the employee may choose to terminate the person's employment. Similarly, if we neglect to fulfill an obligation we explicitly agreed to in some life role, the people who are impacted by the loss may experience dissatisfaction. So the desire to provide a satisfactory performance forms the basis of many obligations, and the desire to serve others.

1

Life Satisfaction

Life satisfaction refers to a person's evaluation with life as a whole, rather than the person's satisfaction with specific physical, mental, or environmental conditions. Researchers attribute a number of factors to life satisfaction including family, career, religiosity, community involvement, and time spent engaging in enjoyable activities. But a person could be dissatisfied with any these specific domains of life satisfaction, like a physical illness, a harmful relationship, dangerous conditions, financial losses, or other negative life experiences, and still have a high level of life satisfaction.

Ruut Veenhoven, a Dutch Sociologist specializing in the study of happiness, pointed out that life satisfaction studies tend to focus on socio-economic differences in which financially deprived citizens enjoy fewer of life's pleasures. But the greatest differences in life satisfaction, he says, are caused by conditions that provoke emotions, like relationships and mental health.[70] The ability to handle life's problems, he added, is a significant contributor to life satisfaction. People have greater life satisfaction when they are physically and mentally healthy, have more energy, better mental resilience, or are socially assertive, empathetic, and open to new experiences. People who were dissatisfied, in contrast, felt they had little control over life events.[71]

At the beginning of this chapter, we briefly looked at how emotions are indicators of personal satisfaction. Psychologists call that a person's subjective wellbeing, or how people feel, emotionally, about their quality of life. Subjective wellbeing includes the frequency by which people experience positive or negative emotions. Improvements in subjective wellbeing were shown, in some studies, to be associated with better health and a longer lifespan.[21]

Personal satisfaction is not only strongly associated with emotions, which indicate satisfaction or dissatisfaction, but to memory and motivation as well. The emotions, themselves, are motivators that shift people's interests toward, or away from, specific activities. If people are particularly unhappy with something in their lives, they may be motivated to change it. Or an exciting activity, like a sports event, may spark an interest in doing it. In the first chapter on motivation, we looked how marketing professionals use emotional branding to attract the interest of potential buyers. Marketers want to show consumers why they would be happier owning a product to attract more interest in owning it. Emotions also direct personal interactions. When interacting with strangers, people may be more inviting toward someone who is pleasurable to be around, or may consider a person who makes them angry, a jerk.

These emotional tendencies are innate, to some extent. An infant, who does not yet have language skills, attributes positive and negative emotions to people and other things depending on whether they are perceived as scary or playful. As people develop language skills, their emotional responses influence how they label things. And the way things are labeled can also evoke an emotional response if it influences a person's satisfaction with those things.

But to understand why the brain is wired this way, we need to look at how memories form, and the formation of learned responses. During the late 19th century, Ivan Pavlov conducted experiments in what is now called Classical Conditioning, which demonstrated how a neural stimulus could be conditioned to produce an involuntary reflex. In one experiment, he associated the sound of a metronome with food, causing a dog to salivate when he heard the sound of a metronome. Certainly many of our natural biological responses, like fear and hunger, are innate and originate in fixed brain structures that all people have in common. But what is different about each person's development, and what makes each person unique, are the types of things they fear and the types of things that make them salivate.

If all behavioral tendencies had genetic origins, and resulted from larger or smaller brain structures, we would expect a person with a phobia to have more or less fear in general. But that does not appear to be the case. A tightrope walker may be afraid of spiders, or a crocodile wrangler may be afraid of heights. Fears tend to be localized to specific things. And those phobias, and similarly disgust of certain foods, seem to be automatic and become hardwired in the brain, but do not necessarily have genetic origins.

In the early decades of the 20th century, John Watson and Rosalie Rayner further explored this idea in a study they conducted on an eleven-month-old child. The child, they called Albert, was introduced to a rat, rabbit, and a monkey. At first, he was unafraid and curious, and sometimes wanted to touch the animals, which became the neutral stimuli in the experiment. When the experimenters surprised Albert by striking a steel bat with a hammer, he began to cry. This act of striking the bat became the unconditioned stimulus.

When the researchers combined the two in repeated

experiments, and struck the bat in the presence of a rat, Albert developed a fear of the rat. In other words, the researchers would present the rat without the sound, and Albert would cry and crawl away. The researchers successfully programmed Albert's brain to fear the rat. Albert's fear also transferred to other animals, an affect they called stimulus generalization. Consequently, Albert developed a phobia of small animals. As he was introduced to them, he would cry and crawl away.[35] Watson and Raynor later concluded that this type of conditioning may continue to influence a person's behavior long after the events occurred.[75]

Just as Albert learned to attach fear and negative emotions to animals, people attach emotions and labels to many things in their lives. Someone becomes a jerk, or an idea becomes a stinking pile of garbage, or a restaurant becomes disgusting. People associate positive emotions and labels to things as well, when specific people become heroes, or lovers, or at least respectable citizens. In our personal relationships, we attribute emotions and labels to the actions of other people, which have an influence on how we interact with them and our sense of obligation to them. Sometimes, how people make us feel has more of an influence on our relationship than what they actually do or say.

Ironically, one of the more remarkable achievements of mankind, the ability to assign words, numbers, and symbols to represent things in the human experience, also causes enormous amounts of disagreement, hatred, and violent conflict. On the one hand, it has enabled people to store and transmit ideas, rapidly develop skills in terms of personal development, and continue to innovate and advance technologies. But people also commit horrifying acts of murder and terrorism because of the emotions and labels they attribute to certain people, or groups of people.

In the movie Hotel Rwanda, which depicted the 1994 Rwandan genocide, the Hutus were in an ongoing civil war with the Tutsi for control of the government. The Hutus used RTLM (or, Hutu Power hate) radio to exacerbate negative emotions about the Tutsi. They called the Tutsi traitors and infidels, and dehumanized them as insects that must be crushed. In short time, the Hutu used the radio as a tool to recruit civilians armed with machetes to slaughter the Tutsi population by the hundreds of thousands, leaving thousands of dead bodies cut to pieces in the streets. Since the 1994 massacre, the Rwandan economy and the nation's tourism industry have recovered. But the events that happened during the genocide are a graphic example of how emotional branding and the labeling of a person or group of people, become a unifying force of hatred within a group.

Emotions and labels influence even the simplest and most common daily decisions. Suppose Monique and her friend Sharon stop at a local restaurant they have dined at for years. Today, something seemed different: The restaurant did not have as much business as usual. When they received their food, Monique's sweat tea was more sour than sweet and the meat on her hamburger was half-raw. The fried chicken on Sharon's sandwich was too hard and crunchy, like it had sat under a heat lamp for three hours. When they informed the manager, who was a young man in his early twenties they had never seen before, he seemed annoyed and offended by the complaint. But he offered to bring them more food. And Monique and Sharon agreed. This incident could be a simple mistake. Maybe the staff is new and is still being trained. But since Monique and Sharon had a negative experience, they did not want to risk dining there again.

People usually do not remember routine one-time experiences in great detail. But studies show that emotionally provocative events, like the birth of a child, or the September 11th attack on the World Trade Center, or any event that evokes extreme pain, sadness, pleasure, or awe, tends to be remembered and recalled more vividly than experiences that do not evoke emotion. One explanation for why may be that people tend to reflect longer on experiences that had a profound, and world-changing, impact on their lives. We think more about those experiences, talk about them, try to explain them, and make a better mental record of the experience, all of which is a deliberate attempt to recall those memories more accurately.

People are also compelled to remember things that are of particular interest to them. If we want to attend an upcoming event, or do not want to forget something, we may remind ourselves in anticipation of the event. Not only do people do this in their private lives, the Press does it when a major event occurs, like when a well known celebrity dies, or when a natural disaster kills dozens of people. Those events tend to be replayed in the media because they are world-changing, impactful, and are of interest to viewers and may be remembered more vividly.

2
The Influence of Gains & Losses

Every decision we make presents the possibility of gaining or losing something we want, whether it is time, a sense of wellbeing, health, safety, trust, acceptance, money, or opportunities. We may be happy with a decision that benefited us, or regret a decision that caused harm. The prospect of making gains, or experiencing losses, has a tremendous influence on our behavior and emotional state, and is often used to motivate people to make purchases, or to incentivize productivity.

Even small gains or losses that do not have monetary exchange value could change a person's overall satisfaction and mood during the day. A few years ago, a colleague of mine began celebrating because he won some coins while playing a video game on his mobile phone. The coins had no practical use or monetary value. But he was ecstatic and filled with joy because he was a winner. We can observe this type of joyful response in the excitement that erupts among fans of the winning team at a sports event. The fans of the losing team, in contrast, may appear to be shocked and emotionally crushed as they hold their faces in horror while witnessing their team's defeat. Rivalry among fans is sometimes so intense and so emotionally charged that fans will fight in the streets as we saw at the Euro 2016 Championship, where police had to fire tear gas and make arrests to stop the fighting between Russian and English football fans.[73]

Gains or losses are also used in business to incentivize productivity. Managers try to motivate and retain employees by providing financial compensation in exchange for labor. In addition to a paycheck, employers may provide other benefits that increase an employee's willingness to work, like the opportunity to develop skills, gain experience, or develop positive relationships. If workers feel that they have something more to gain that improves their job satisfaction, they may have greater reason to stay and cooperate in terms of supplying their labor, which may further make the organization more productive.

Gains and losses not only influence our drive, motivation, and ambitions, but our sense of fairness and justice. Consider a time when a possession of yours was lost or stolen. Maybe you felt anger or regret. That anger stems from the human biology's own natural defenses that compels people to protect their interests, to avoid losing the things they want. This sense of fairness or unfairness is learned at a very early age. When a child receives a toy that another child did not, the unlucky child may be unhappy and may cry because of the perceived unfairness. That perception of fairness largely depends on what people agree to, in terms of what they gain and must give up, and whether they are satisfied with the outcome.

People differ by culture in their perception of what is fair and just. During the 1950s in the United States, a prevalent cultural norm was that the wife stayed home and took care of the family and home, while the husband earned an income. At the time, many men and women considered that gender based division of labor natural and acceptable. But since that time, women have become more independent. And many women in the United States view the expectation to become a stay-at-home wife as a loss of rights and opportunities.

This need for fairness is the whole reason for contract law, and the reason people form agreements. If you work for an employer, you may have signed a document that provides your employer and yourself with protections about pay and the possession of company assets to prevent either party from experiencing unacceptable losses. Or if you purchased an expensive piece of electronics, you may have purchased a warranty that guarantees replacement if the item is damaged within a certain amount of time. Or maybe you made an agreement with a neighbor that her teenage child will not be throwing loud and crazy parties at three o'clock in the morning. All of these agreements protect those involved from unfair losses, like the loss of sleep, which guarantees a certain amount of satisfaction.

In a fair exchange, both parties agree to the terms of the exchange. But when one person gains at the expense of another, like in the crime of theft, the victim did not agree to the loss. And when people experience losses they did not agree to, they are more likely to be dissatisfied, and may be motivated to restore equity. When people are threatened by robberies and shootings in crumbling urban areas that have high crime rates, they may be more likely to express a greater sense of unfairness and fearfulness because they are frequently exposed to potential losses to their physical and financial wellbeing.

In uncivilized societies where racial or ethnic discrimination is allowed, people unfairly lose opportunities, and sometimes their safety, because of their race or ethnicity. Other types of losses, like the loss of a career, or the loss of a family member, are significant and un-restorable because they provide a significant amount of support that may be difficult, if not impossible, to replace. And when people are responsible for those losses, government services could help to restore a sense of fairness by enforcing laws to prevent further losses, or by providing civil services to recover from the loss.

3
Economic Influences

In capital markets, producer and consumer behaviors are influenced by personal satisfaction more than any other factor. The whole reason markets exist in the first place is to satisfy the demand for goods or services. When the buyer and seller are both satisfied with an exchange, they are made better off.

The market price of the product tends to be influenced by supply and demand (i.e., the product's scarcity and how much people want it). But the actual price is determined by fair market value, which is the price the buyer and seller finally agree upon, depending on how much the buyer wants the item, or how much the seller wants to sell the item. In the end, both have to be sufficiently satisfied with what they receive in return before they agree to the exchange.

Personal satisfaction influences consumer and producer behaviors in other ways. If we are dissatisfied with what we have, we may be motivated to replace it. Or if something appears to be better than what we currently possess, we may be motivated to purchase it. Marketers try to tap into this deeper desire by showing us how a product will make us happier, how it solves a problem, or makes our lives more convenient. By showing us what we gain by purchasing a product, marketers are using the influence of gains to change people's buying behaviors.

From the producer or supplier perspective, the seller's ability to satisfy a buyer's demand for a good or service, determines whether the seller stays profitable. Any decrease in customer satisfaction may lead to a decline in demand for a product, especially when the same product is available elsewhere. That's why managers sometimes establish a return policy, to refund customers who are dissatisfied with a purchase. They know that losing a customer would cost more in terms of repeat purchases than the money lost from the refund. At the same time, the seller must be satisfied with the profits made from sales or the seller would have no incentive to stay in business.

Economic conditions have an influence on personal satisfaction in other ways. According to some studies, people who live in economically prosperous conditions report experiencing more life satisfaction than people living in poorer conditions.[15] A Pew Research Center survey found that people with more education, employment, income, and household goods, experienced greater satisfaction than people without those things. The survey looked at whether the participants had specific household goods, like a "television, refrigerator, washing machine, microwave oven, computer, car, bicycle, motorcycle/scooter and radio." Many of these, like the car or washing machine, are conveniences that reduce the burden and workload of living, and enable people to spend more time enjoying life. The greater number of items the participants possessed, the greater amount of happiness they reported experiencing. But the participants also said that some things were more important than financial prosperity, like "health, their children's education and being safe from crime."[56]

Increasing material wealth does not always translate into increased happiness. A study published in 2010 from Princeton University concluded that, in the United States, people are made happier as their income increased to about $75,000 annually. Beyond that income, they were not made happier.[44] The pursuit of material wealth, it appears, has diminishing returns in terms of producing greater life satisfaction as people approach a certain level of income. Once they achieve that income, they seem to have overcome the financial deficiencies and living conditions that would create dissatisfaction, like not having enough for living expenses.

Even the pursuit of material wealth, by itself, could lead to dissatisfaction. When people work harder and longer hours, employers and clients demand more of their time, labor, and attention, which may lead to unhealthy stress and unhealthy lifestyle habits. People who are driven to be successful in their careers may borrow large amounts of money to pay for an expensive education, and put a significant amount of pressure on themselves to learn more, and be better professionals, while paying down their debt. Married couples who place a high value on financial gains may start arguments and conflicts over financial concerns and potential losses. They may blame each other or harbor resentment over financial losses. And those feelings may lead to more conflicts that increase stress and put a strain on the relationship.

4

Political Influences

Studies have shown that human populations differ, in terms of the happiness of their citizens in different parts of the world, suggesting that government officials may be able to improve the overall satisfaction of citizens by investing in community projects. Even then, any population will have a natural rate of dissatisfaction among citizens, since life satisfaction is influence by more than politics or living conditions. Life satisfaction is also influenced by genes, chemistry, stress, disease, social interactions, aging, and life experiences. Some people have neurological disorders, substance use disorders, or other mental disorders that influence their life satisfaction. So separating personal conditions that create dissatisfaction from poor political or environmental conditions, would require additional research and analysis.

Government officials in some nations proactively study the satisfaction of their citizens. The nation of Bhutan, for example, measures the life satisfaction of citizens with a Gross National Happiness (GNH) Index to understand what specific conditions cause dissatisfaction among citizens. The GNH is calculated using nine domains of life satisfaction. One of those is psychological wellbeing, which includes a person's life satisfaction and emotional state. Others include health and time use, education, cultural diversity, performance of government, community vitality, and environmental responsibility. Citizens are also asked about their standard of living, which is comprised of their income, assets, and housing.[14]

Government officials may also be able to improve satisfaction among citizens by studying the health, crime, and the conditions of life in a population, to identify the common causes of citizens' dissatisfaction and create programs aimed at solving those problems. Veenhoven even suggested that measures of life satisfaction could be used to assess the effectiveness of policy on quality of life.[70] Conditions that are not ideal, but are mostly acceptable, he said, may provide for a quality of life that leads to more life satisfaction. Low satisfaction, on the other hand, indicates something is wrong and may indicate the need for further investigation into the actual cause.[72]

Quality of life refers to the collective attributes that comprise a person's mental or physical condition, along with anything that would have an effect on that condition, like societal and environmental factors. Quality of life is not the same as standard of living, which refers to wealth in financial and material resources. Some factors that influence quality of life include access to healthy food, clean air, clean water, protection from toxic chemicals, and protection from social problems.[60]

When a city is plagued by urban decay, a crumbling infrastructure, pollution, a lack of employment, or crime, people have reasons to be fearful and dissatisfied. When people fear for their safety, or have few job opportunities, low income, or difficulty commuting, those experiences influence their expectations about the future and their outlook on life. Citizens who are significantly discontented with the political establishment as a result of food shortages, or being denied basic rights have, historically, started violent political revolutions. So, when government officials finance programs to build and maintain public infrastructure, remove pollution and urban decay, improve public safety, and attract business and entertainment, citizens have fewer reasons to complain about the prevailing political establishment and have more reasons to be satisfied.

CHAPTER IV:
PRODUCTIVITY

Productivity is a measure of the amount of work performed. In business, productivity is a measure of output, in terms of the amount of goods or services produced. But in our private lives, we could measure productivity in terms of the amount of time and energy we spend working towards achieving a goal. Outcomes tend to be gained or lost depending on the amount of work put in. Not enough productivity and we fall short of our goals. But some goals are more challenging than others. And a person could spend an enormous amount of time and effort striving to achieve a difficult goal and have nothing to show for it. And later in this chapter, we look at ways of mitigating that risk.

In the last chapter, we looked at the fact that people are motivated to be productive because they want to change the things in their lives they are dissatisfied with. Those things may consist of their living or working conditions, their skills and abilities, or just about anything else in life they want to improve. In this chapter, we look at how to deal with the limited constraints on doing that, in terms of time, opportunity, and the available resources.

1
Vision & Creativity

Figuring out how to shape your life starts with vision and seeing the future you want to create. And you could start by imagining the life you want, and defining what success looks like in terms of creating that life. But whatever you imagine, the task of actually making that mental vision into reality requires creativity, strategy, and commitment.

Creativity is a process of envisioning what is missing in a picture or an arrangement, and trying to fill in that void. Gestalt psychology shows us that the brain does this automatically when it fills in the missing details in perception to create a more organized, meaningful, and complete picture of reality. But people also do it in their deliberate thinking when drawing from the palette of their own interests to envision the lives they want to pursue and how to turn that vision into reality.

Making new discoveries is an essential part of the creative process because you do not know what you have to be creative with until you discover it. As you acquire more, in terms of experiences, exposure, and knowledge, you have more to work with. If you want to remodel your living space, you may discover new ways of doing that by drawing from existing examples for ideas. Imitation, and copying the work of a satisfactory example, innovating an existing creation, and adding value, helps in the creative process to create satisfactory work. Other types of discoveries are made by talking to people, searching, researching, and discovering new opportunities, useful tools, and new ideas.

Using these techniques to be more creative is useful in social and business life. If you want to organize a party for a coworker, you may contemplate questions like: What would it look like, would you decorate, and what food would you serve? Maybe the party should be a themed party, or should be located at your coworker's favorite restaurant. What is missing from the party that needs to be creatively fill-in?

The creative urge to fill-in the perceived voids in our lives also compels us to recognize and solve problems, and fill-in the blanks of missing knowledge about things we are curious about. Just about any behavior we look at, whether it is completely absurd, like laughing at the antics of a comedian, or a drug addiction that nearly destroys a person's life, fills-in some void. Even activities that would be considered unremarkable, when taking an afternoon walk around the block, when satiating our hunger for food, or when engaging in a conversation that fills an awkward silence, provides repletion, and fills-in the perceived lacunas (or voids) in our lives. This perceived incompleteness is the source of all wants, desires, and necessity, and is the motivating inspiration for our life-goals, to make our life-work more satisfactory and complete.

Even adapting to new circumstances is a creative process. Just as other life forms exhibit a manifold of characteristics and features that give them greater biotic potential; we develop traits that give us greater potential in pursuing and protecting our interests. As we respond to people, and the demands of our environment, we develop helpful traits that become strengths, skills, and competencies, which provide us with greater abilities in the circumstances we face.

2
Strategy

Managing a livelihood is not necessarily like a business with the ultimate goal of making a profit. Not all behavior is economic or has financial ends. But each person is a manager, decision maker, and owner of a life, livelihood, and personal estate. And each person makes decisions about how to use time and resources, and everything available, to create a life. Being successful at doing those things depends on strategy, managing the execution of that strategy, and solving the problems standing in the way of making that mental vision a reality.

The first part of that strategy involves establishing the goals that need to be achieved. If Jillian wants to be a winning athlete, then showing up to a competition and trying her best will not ensure victory. To be competitive, she needs to practice, exercise, test her abilities, and measure her progress by comparing her results against those of other athletes. She needs to create a strategy for how to achieve her longer-term goals or she will certainly fail. And that planning usually starts by breaking down longer-term goals into simpler, more manageable, shorter-term goals, or what could be called proximate goals and milestones. The path to success may begin by achieving daily, weekly, monthly, or yearly goals that develop into habits and routine activities that you do regularly.

All of this work requires making time. When people have limited and targeted goals, maybe they want to learn a language, it is possible to make time for that activity. Making time is similar to making space. If you have no more space in a room, then you have two options: You can scoot everything closer together, or remove half the items. When you have done that, you have made space. Time is similar in that you can work faster, or sacrifice certain opportunities, to pursue more desirable goals or ambitions.

3

Opportunity Costs

When people consider how to spend their limited time, they are forced to consider opportunity costs, which consist of what they give up, in terms of time, money, and other opportunities, to get what they want. People cannot always have everything they want because of limitations in time, cognitive ability, and information. Herbert Simon called that limitation in human capacity bounded rationality, which forces us to accept satisfactory outcomes, rather than ideal outcomes. And since we cannot always have everything we want, we are forced to give up some things to get other things, even if that means sacrificing something you really enjoy, like giving up junk food to live a healthier lifestyle.

Today, many young people are forgoing the opportunity to marry, at least in the near term, to pursue a career. According to a U.S. Census Bureau survey, during 1970 most people in the United States were married by the age of 24. But today, the majority of U.S. citizens delay marriage until after that age. The reason for this, the researchers concluded, is that more than twice as many women are attending college, pursuing careers, and seeking financial independence.[1]

Every moment we spend doing something has an opportunity cost. An Economist may call that a sunk cost, which is a necessary loss that we are not able to get back and should not regret. Whether we think the cost is worth it depends on our satisfaction with what we gain in return. To illustrate this idea, imagine Tim is a 16-year-old young man trying to save money for a vehicle. During the weekend, he has two options: He could work at the restaurant around the corner from where he lives, or he could play video games with his friends. If he plays games, he gives up the money he would earn at the restaurant. In other words, Tim pays the same amount of money he could earn at the restaurant to play games for two days. Does this make sense if Tim is never able to afford a vehicle that could drive him to an even higher paying job?

To be fair, the argument could be made that people are happier when they spend their money on experiences, like playing games or going to a sports event, rather than on possessions. According to a study by Ryan Howell at San Francisco State University, and Thomas Gilovich at Cornell University, the happiness experienced from purchasing a possession fades over time, while the happiness from an experience may be recalled from memory. Family and friends are often included in those experiences. And those experiences may be shared with other people in conversations or in social media. Gilovich pointed out that these findings are another reason policy makers should consider creating programs that create opportunities for positive experiences in the community, like creating bike trails and parks.[43]

Weighing the opportunity costs of working rather than having fun certainly does not make our choices any easier. Maybe the optimal choice balances the two options and sacrifice some fun for work. After living expenses are paid and some discretionary income is saved, you have more choices about what to buy, where to go, and have more time to pursue your interests.

4

Risk Tolerance

Risk is in everything you do. Every decision you make, whether it is in your relationships, employment, traveling, or in the pursuit of new opportunities, presents uncertainty and the risk of loss. In every business transaction, the buyer or seller risks losing money. And anytime you give up something to get something, you risk losing something in the process. All people face varying degrees of risk in life. The majority of decisions, like purchasing an item at the supermarket, present low risk because you stand to lose very little.

And people are aware of those risks and have a desire to protect themselves from loss and avoid unknown and potentially negative outcomes. But when a person develops a habit of always doing that, the person becomes risk-averse. Risk-aversion is more common when a person is unsure about a decision because of inexperience, which increases the risk of failure. When a person has low confidence in one's ability to perform an activity, that person may avoid that activity all together.

The problem with avoiding all forms of risk is that it does not help to create the outcomes that people want. People must have some risk-tolerance, and be willing to accept some loss and failure, when trying to create the outcomes they want. Consider an entrepreneur who invests in the land, labor, and capital necessary to become a manufacturer, and then tries to make that business profitable. That entrepreneur is accepting a significant amount of risk, in terms of potential financial losses and bankruptcy. Some people are willing to risk everything, even their safety or livelihood, for a career, business venture, or political cause they value and believe in. But those pursuits could also lead to unnecessary losses and hardship if those risks are not mitigated.

5
Risk Mitigation

Risk mitigation is a process of making potential losses less severe, which is not the same thing as risk avoidance. People must tolerate some risk to achieve their goals and create the lives they want. But those risks, and the potential losses, may be reduced by using techniques for recognizing and reducing uncertainty, and increasing the likelihood of achieving your goals.

The first technique is to avoid unnecessary risk. Some people take on more risk than they need, or take on fruitless endeavors, and end up with nothing to show for their time and effort. A smart risk, and a realistic goal, is one that has a great deal of certainty in achieving, like a smaller, more manageable, task. In other words, setting the bar low makes all of the hurdles in the way of achieving your goals easier to overcome, and confirms your ability to overcome those challenges before moving onto more difficult ones. Consequently, you are more confident and certain about your success on a more consistent basis, and you build a track record of success as you make marginal gains toward longer-term goals. Trying to be successful at riskier pursuits that involve an indeterminate amount of time and uncertainty has a greater potential for failure and unwanted loss.

You could also mitigate risk by not investing too much in ventures that depend on luck and chance where the probabilities of creating the outcomes you want are low. If a decision results in one of two possible outcomes, then the probability of achieving your goal is the same as a coin flip, which is close to .5, or 50 percent. As you increase the number of possible outcomes, assuming the result depends on chance, the probability of creating the outcome you want goes down. Gambling and criminal activities are examples of risky enterprises that depend on luck and chance, and have a high probability of failure.

Another risk mitigation technique involves overestimating what will be required to create a desired outcome. Project managers sometimes slightly overestimate the amount of time or money a project will take to finish because of unforeseen challenges that make the project overdue or over budget. When making capacity planning decisions, it's better to have too much capacity, rather than falling short. If city planners wanted to reduce the chances of flooding or water rationing, they could create a greater abundance of channels and reservoirs, and require builders to slope surfaces to divert rain water into those channels to harvest rain water.

Entrepreneurs mitigate risk by trying to minimize potential losses and maximize profits as much as possible. One way of doing that is by ensuring some guaranteed demand for the business's goods or services. And that largely depends on whether an adequate amount of demand exists in a market, and whether buyers are satisfied with the business's goods or services, and how well existing competition satisfies demand.

6

Commitment

A person's commitment to achieving a personal or organizational goal consists of what that person is willing to do, or sacrifice, in terms of making time and expending energy to achieve that goal. How committed the person is to achieving the goal may ultimately determine the person's success. Within organizations, management may be able use techniques to increase the commitment of workers to achieve the organization's strategic goals.

In an earlier chapter, we looked at how management may be able to motivate workers by providing more than just a paycheck, by increasing their job satisfaction. In *Smarter Faster Better: The Secrets of Being Productive in Life and Business*, Charles Duhigg adds that management may be able to increase the commitment of workers by giving them more control, and more say, in how the organization operates. People are generally more motivated, he argues, when they perceive greater control over the outcome, and are less motivated when they have little, or no, control over the outcome.[25] When people have more control over an outcome, they are more likely to do it. And when the effort appears to be impossible, futile, and hopeless, it leads to giving up. Psychologists refer to the latter condition as learned helplessness, which is a condition we look at in a later chapter on mental disorders.

One way of giving workers a greater sense of control is by giving them a voice in how the organization operates. Empowering workers gives them a since of ownership in the operation, and enables them to identify deficiencies and problems in how the organization operates that could be improved. Providing workers with training, supplies, and the help necessary to do the job, gives them a greater sense of control by reducing dysfunction, and enables them to perform at a higher level when serving their clients. And when workers have fewer problems and fewer frustrations in performing their job, their job satisfaction may improve.

A decline of commitment within an organization may occur for a number of reasons, starting with conflicts of interest (i.e., employees who put their own interests before the organization's). Personal beliefs, differences in opinion, stress, and conflicts, cause dysfunction when people refuse to communicate, or work, with each other. Dysfunction and organizational inefficiency occurs when people focus more on their own opinions, dislike, and disagreements, rather than the organizational goals or the outcomes they are trying to create.

Sometimes too much commitment leads to disastrous outcomes when time and money continues to be invested in losing propositions. Behavioral scientists call this tendency an escalation of commitment, in which continued investment in a failing pursuit is justified by the amount of time and money already spent toward achieving a goal. These types of pursuits are often initiated as a result of poor planning, a lack of information about the investment required, a lack of expertise, and being overly confident in the ability to achieve a goal within an unrealistic amount of time and expense.

CHAPTER V:
CONDITIONING

People have a variety of ways to improve their mental and physical condition. An athlete makes a performance improvement by repeating an activity, like running or lifting weights. And people are able to make behavioral changes by repeating activities that develop new habits, skills, and improve abilities. As a person repeatedly tests and improves an ability, confidence in that ability increases, and the person gains greater self-confidence when confronting challenges requiring the ability.

Successfully performing a task frequently improves a person's proficiency, competency, and overall fitness at performing the task. Testing a person's ability to recall details about a subject, tests the person's mental retention, and how strong that person's knowledge of the subject is. Each of these are attributes of a person's mental condition that may be improved. And this chapter looks at how to further improve those attributes with conditioning, in addition to how people improve their self-confidence, and the positive and negative influences on childhood development.

1
The Principle of Conditioning

Conditioning is a process of affecting change in the condition of something as a result of repeated reinforcement. Beyond genes and other biochemical influences, conditioning may be the most significant influence on personality development. And the idea that a behavior can gradually strengthen, applies to almost all people with a few exceptions. Some people have disabilities or impairments due to birth defects or the aging process that prevent them from learning. But even then, most people are able to learn, and improve their mental performance, in just about any condition and during any stage of life.

The Principle of Conditioning, in its vaguest form, suggests that the more we do something, the better we get at it. During childhood development, this fundamental principle underlies the development of motor skills, cognitive development, and speaking abilities. It is responsible for behavioral adaptation as people develop responses to routine circumstances that strengthen with repeated exposure to specific social and environmental conditions. And as people perform those routine activities, they tend to become more proficient and habitual until the behavior becomes automatic and second nature.

In the chapter on satisfaction, we looked at how experiments by Ivan Pavlov and John Watson demonstrate that the human brain attaches emotions and labels to things in the environment. This passive form of learning that results from repeated exposure to specific conditions can alter a person's mental state and frame of mind. When a person is exposed to prolonged adverse experiences, for example, that type of conditioning could lead to a mental disorder. Some examples include soldiers who develop Post Traumatic Stress Disorder (PTSD) resulting from extended exposure to combat, or victims of abusive relationships who develop emotional disorders.

But not all human behavior is the result of an unthinking involuntary reflex to external stimuli. We not only have a limbic system that compels us react to our surroundings; we have a cortex that enables us to learn, think, and reason. In contrast to passive mode of learning, in which a person's mental condition changes as a result of exposure to environmental circumstances, people are able to actively learn to operate in new ways, develop new skills, and improve self-confidence.

2

Changing the Brain

The brain naturally changes as people age. But the development of new cognitive abilities has limitations. Genetic factors play a significant role in limiting our potential, in terms of our mental and physical abilities. Shorter people may not be the greatest basketball players. Extremely tall people may not make the fastest horse jockeys. And even when they are talented in their sport, those traits tend to be a disadvantage.

In a similar way, brain anatomy has a significant influence on personality development. In fact, the size of certain brain structures may influence the expression of specific behaviors. A study conducted at Stanford University School of Medicine in 2013 found that children who experience more fear, anxiety, and stress had a larger Amygdala, which is a brain structure associated with regulating fear and emotion.[8]

Some reasons for why brain structures may be larger or smaller than average may include genes, brain injury, an infection, or some other biological condition. When we look at an fMRI scan, we see that blood flow to certain areas of the brain increases with activity, just as blood flow to muscles increases when they are in use. And those differences become more obvious when comparing a healthy, active, and more developed prefrontal cortex, with one that is not as developed. Superficial appearances alone do not really tell us whether a brain structure is larger because of frequent stimulation and use, or because of some other genetic or biological factor.

People do not have a choice about their genes, unless they undergo gene therapy. But people do have a choice about the amount they work, learn, and practice certain activities, which lends itself to mental fitness at performing specific tasks. And people are able to create new memories and develop new mental functionality just as they are able to build muscle with engagement and repetition.

For some time, scientists have known that engaging in mentally stimulating activities improves cognitive abilities, brain function, and fitness. And studies suggest that, to a limited extent, eating a nutritious diet, and engaging in physical exercise, increases oxygen and nutrients to the brain, improves brain composition, brain function, and brain health. New brain functions, and even destroyed brain functions, may be built and rebuilt as a result of the brain's neuroplasticity (i.e., the brain's ability to form new neural connections).

Norman Doidge explored this idea in his book the *Brain That Changes Itself*, in which he looks at the history, science, case studies, and applications of neuroplasticity.[22] He describes stories of people who have experienced severe brain damage that caused a loss of significant functionality, like the ability to walk or communicate. And instead of regaining that functionality as a result of surgery, or the brain healing itself, the patients used repetitive exercises for an extended period of time to slowly build new neural connections that bypass the damaged ones. A person with a learning disability, like difficulty reading, was able to build new neural connections that provided new mental functionality.

That type of change is extremely slow because it requires hardwiring new neural connections. The process tends to produce slight, marginal, changes that occur over a very long period of time, and consumes a great deal of time, energy, and freedom from other interesting activities. But it is possible. And it is often preceded by a process that we explore in the next section, which may not only be applied to personal development, but to the development of organizations as well.

3

Empirical Discovery

The two forms of learning attributed to human development are the transmission of knowledge and empirical discovery. Education mostly teaches by the transmission of knowledge, which is able to rapidly develop a student's knowledge about a subject. But we never truly know what we are capable of doing until we test our abilities. And that is an act of empirical discovery, which is an act of learning by doing and engaging and, specifically, by seeing what we are capable of.

Scientific research relies on empirical discovery in the form of experimentation and testing hypothesis to learn about what is possible or impossible in nature, and usually in a controlled laboratory environment. Researchers are able to solve complex problems by trial and error, using experimentation, testing possibilities, and building on existing discoveries. Similarly, each of us is a scientist of our own potential, discovering what is possible in our own lives. Our abilities and self-control are continuously being tested by everyday challenges, big and small. And even our ideas, conclusions, and theories, are continuously being tested to see if they contain truth and validity.

As we spend more time pursuing our unique interests, we become more mentally fit and specialized in performing some activities more than others. And while genes may give us an advantage in performing certain types of tasks, genes are not entirely responsible for talent. A participant in a memory competition once said that he was able to memorize a deck of cards within a minute, not because he was genetically special, but because he repeatedly tested himself and slowly developed his talent over a long period of time.

People could even use the process of conditioning to improve their wellbeing. This does not occur merely by thinking positively, or mentally going to their happy place, but instead by making time for experiences and activities that change their emotional state. Actively participating in games and recreational activities that elicit pleasurable emotions may, in the short term, reinforce pleasurable experiences, create pleasurable memories, and provide some immunity from conditions that would, otherwise, cause a decline in wellbeing.

Empirical discovery is applicable to just about any area of human development. Consider rejection therapy, in which a participant actively seeks out rejection to desensitize the fear of rejection. Sometimes when participants expect to be rejected, they are not. And, instead, they are allowed to do something they did not think they could do. Testing our abilities this way, helps us to overcome the perceived barriers in our lives and accomplish things we did not know we could accomplish. And it helps to improve self-confidence and outlook on life.

4

Self-Confidence

Achieving any goal requires enough confidence in the ability to be successful. B. F. Skinner wrote about how a tennis player practices until he achieves a certain level of consistency in his game. And that frequent reinforcement "builds faith" in his abilities, and builds confidence in his success.[62] Alfred Adler gave another example of how a marathon runner who does not "trust himself" to hurdle an obstacle, tries to avoid it.[2]

Confidence in certain abilities, whether those abilities

are intellectual, physical, or social, is built by trial and error. Trying a new activity presents the risk of failure. But once we try and are successful, we increase certainty, and build confidence, in our ability to do it again. A college once told me about his son who took up sky diving. At first, he was terrified to jump and did not think he could bring himself to do it. But after his first jump, sky diving became his new favorite past-time, and he could not get enough of it. When a person gains greater confidence in performing an activity, that person may become more eager and motivated to do it. And the activity may develop into an ongoing interest and passion.

As our abilities are tested, our successes and failures provide us with feedback, which influences our confidence in those abilities. Suppose Tim decides he wants to run a marathon. A few days before the marathon, he runs two miles, becomes exhausted, and gives up. Naturally, Tim would lose confidence in his ability to run the entire marathon that weekend. And that is why testing our abilities keeps us honest, at least with ourselves, about our abilities. But it also gives us the opportunity to recognize and overcome deficiencies in our performance, if we choose to.

To become a stronger speaker, it's not enough to read and memorize a speech. The speech must be performed to reduce uncertainty about whether it will be delivered as expected. When an inventor creates a new invention on paper, that inventor never really knows for certain that the invention will work as expected until it is tested. And the same is true with knowledge and abilities: Those abilities must be tested to make sure they perform as expected before a person can have real certainty and real confidence. The more a person performs and observes the strength of those abilities, the more feedback the person receives from successes and failures, and the more opportunities that person has to improve.

If you remember back to a time when you had an upcoming test, and you quizzed yourself to see if you could answer the questions as you studied, then you had some idea of how well you would do on the test. If you could answer all the questions, then you had a high level of confidence in your ability to pass the exam. Psychologists call this the testing effect. Reading material multiple times does not ensure you are able to recall that material at a later time. But if you test your ability to recall the material as you read it, you confirm that you are actually learning it. And studies have also shown that recalling knowledge after an extended period of time further improves long-term knowledge retention.[59]

The idea that people are able to build confidence in certain abilities by testing those abilities and gradually improving them, not only applies to developing self-confidence, it applies to building confidence within teams and organizations. Having confidence that an organization will perform as expected requires testing that organization, to see how well it performs, and where improvements could be made. Testing specific abilities, and measuring performance, provides management with the opportunity to identify and prevent failures, hold workers accountable, and reward strong performance.

Having confidence that anything will perform as expected requires testing it. Goods or services need to be tested and checked for quality and consistency to make sure they are delivered as expected. Some professionals may require rigorous testing to make sure they meet certain requirements in professional competency. Software Developers continuously test their programs as the code them to make sure they are functioning as expected. Prosecutors or Defense Attorneys may test evidence collected at a crime scene, or from witness testimony, to prove or disprove a case. And cities test emergency systems to have confidence they will function as expected.

5
Agents of Encouragement

Early childhood development is one of the more common applications of conditioning. During that time, children develop qualities, like self-confidence, that may influence the entire course of their lives in dramatic ways. In fact, a child's self-confidence may be more a factor in personal and financial success than intelligence. People who are confident in their abilities usually have the grit and tenacity to continue making an effort until the desired result is achieved. They may have better mental resilience during difficult times, the ability to overcome challenges, and a better outlook on life. Lacking that confidence, in contrast, would be discouraging and may lead to giving up.

Responsibility for a child's development begins with the caregiver and ultimately ends with the child once the child grows into adulthood. When the child is young, caregivers make decisions for the child as a way of guiding the child's development, like keeping the child safe and helping the child to make better decisions. Caregivers only have a certain amount of influence on a child's development. Much of the child's development will always be beyond the caregiver's ability to control since it is the product of child's own interests. Personality development is truly a self-creative process in which the child draws partly from the influences and ideas present in the environs, and partly from the palette of one's own innate predispositions, knowledge, and choices to create a unique self.

Parents are able to nudge and encourage a child to make certain choices. But the child must ultimately want to make those choices, rather than being forced or coerced. As Emile Durkheim put it, "the rule prescribing such behavior must be freely desired, that is to say, freely accepted; and this willing acceptance is nothing less than an enlightened assent."[26] Children, like adults, must be convinced that making one choice over another is in their best interests before they will truly want to do it. And a care-giver's ability to do that, along with the ability to encourage greater confidence in the child's abilities, may be much more influential to the child's development than time spent together, social pressure, threats, or bribery.

According to Social Learning Theory, children look to other people for help and guidance and learn to imitate their behavior when trying to solve life problems. During the 1960's, Albert Bandura, Dorothea Ross, and Sheila Ross, at Stanford University studied how aggressive and non-aggressive role models influence the behavior of children. The results suggested that children who were assigned the aggressive role models exhibited aggressive behaviors. Those aggressive behaviors were not observed in the children who were not assigned a role model, or those who were assigned the non-aggressive role model.[36]

What their research tells us is that children learn by example when they have no other source of guidance to influence their behavior. But learning by example may be the worst form of guidance if the child is surrounded by bad examples. When a child has no other form of guidance to draw from and looks to other people as examples, that child will not develop the ability to think independently and be self-guiding.

Encouraging a child to take on challenges that develop cognitive or physical abilities is a better form of guidance that helps to build the child's self-confidence. Caregivers are able to encourage the development of the child's intellect, social skills, and problem solving skills. Repeatedly testing those abilities provides the caregiver with the opportunity to encourage, or discourage, certain types of behaviors, and strengthen responses that will be useful to the child later in life. The child may learn to tolerate personal differences, make friends, be helpful, communicate clearly, trust certain people, learn to recall details, solve challenging problems, and engage in healthy activities. The more the child participates in those activities, the more self-confidence the child has, enabling the child to think more independently, which could improve the child's outlook later in life.

6
Agents of Adversity

Studies have shown that people who had a greater number of adverse childhood experiences have an increased risk of depression, heart disease, and headaches.[64] But observing the causes of those conditions is not so easy. A strong and healthy person may experience a particularly traumatic event and not be significantly affected by it. And most adolescents face some form of adversity, disapproval, conflict, or punishment, and develop interests that conflict with their caregiver's attempt to keep them safe. They may have parents that, on occasion, say or do something that seems mean or cruel. And they do not develop mental disorders or destructive habits.

So seeing how mental disorders have origins in childhood adversity is not easy. And it may be even more difficult to understand how abuse within a family could go undetected by family and friends. People tend to make intuitive judgments based on appearances, what they already know, and whether they have a reason to suspect abuse.

We know that prolonged exposure to adverse experiences, like combat conditions, causes mental disorders, like Post Traumatic Stress Disorder (PTSD). Since those disorders have environmental origins rather than genetic origins, they have the potential to atrophy overtime, sometimes taking years, if the person is living or working in a supportive environment. But even that can create complications if the person has behavioral problems resulting from a severe mental disorder. In terms of childhood adversity, changing the environment could be the difference between a young adult who is healthy, well-adjusted, and academically successful, or a young adult with developmental, emotional, or substance abuse problems that may require law enforcement intervention.

Part of the problem is that the root causes of childhood adversity and behavioral problems have many variations and are complex. Teenage parents who have unintended pregnancies, according to the U.S. Department of Health and Human Services, have "reduced educational attainment and employment opportunity, greater welfare dependency, and increased potential for child abuse and neglect."[17] "Teenage mothers are less likely to get or stay married, less likely to complete high school or college, and more likely to require public assistance and to live in poverty than their peers who are not mothers"..."The infants may be at greater risk of child abuse, neglect, and behavioral and educational problems at later stages."[17]

Behavioral problems may also be caused by birth defects that are not necessarily genetic or chromosomal, but may be caused by teratogens, which are substances, like alcohol, specific drugs, chemicals, and infections that are preventable.[46] Low birth weight, in which a child is born weighing less than 5.5 pounds, is sometimes caused by cigarette smoking, alcohol or illegal drugs, insufficient pregnancy weight, and multiple births. Low birth weight babies are at greater risk of "long-term disabilities, such as cerebral palsy, autism, mental retardation, vision and hearing impairments, and other developmental disabilities."[18] Fetal alcohol syndrome, which is caused by the mother's alcohol consumption during pregnancy, causes poor coordination, developmental disabilities, hyperactivity, psychiatric problems, and criminal behaviors.[13]

Problems in child development also occur as a result of severe adversity from a parent or pier, who continues to mistreat the child on a regular, usually daily, basis. Child maltreatment may exist in the form of physical abuse, sexual abuse, child exploitation and corruption, emotional abuse, and neglect. Emotional abuse is known to cause problems with a child's conduct, as well as cognitive disorders, affective disorders, and other mental disorders. Forms of emotional abuse may include calling the child something other than his or her name. The caregiver may verbally assault the child by ridiculing, verbally threatening, belittling, or bullying. The caregiver may terrorize the child by creating unrealistic expectations and threatening the child if he or she doesn't live up to those expectations. The caregiver may isolate the child, to prevent the child from interacting with other people, which could reveal the abuse. Children who are emotionally abused characteristically have persistent feelings of insecurity, problems forming relationships, a low self-worth, and self-destructive behaviors.[4]

Caregivers sometimes unintentionally become agents of adversity when they create too much conflict with a child, and the conflict becomes mutually reinforcing and continues to escalate and grow worse. Child maltreatment is not the same as a caregiver enforcing rules, or a single angry outburst. But some forms of corporal punishment, like spanking, may become abusive if the parent continues to increase the punishment if the child does not respond accordingly. This is especially true if the caregiver has a mental disorder, or a habit of inflicting uncontrollable violence and hostility toward the child. That type of hostility may provoke the child to do the opposite. Rather than changing an unwanted behavior, the child's instinct is to avoid, or cease to be receptive to, the attackers. The child may fight in protest, and disapprove of the attacks to get them to stop. Frequent occurrences may cause the development of similar behaviors in how the child responds, not only to parents, but to other people.

The child's brain, including the child's emotional, intellectual, or communication skills, is still in the process of forming. And children do not have the experience to know the long-term consequences of their decisions. So they try to stop conflict by fighting or fleeing, by avoiding, or counter-attacking, the aggressor. And if caregivers continue to perpetuate the conflict, the child's counter-attacks and rebellion may grow so exaggerated overtime that they develop into criminal behaviors. In those circumstances, rather than attacking the bad behavior, and arguing, criticizing, or threatening punishment, focusing on ideas and activities that lead to better life outcomes would be more productive and helpful to the child.

In the last section, we looked at how positive reinforcement helps children to develop into strong and independent adults. Negative reinforcement, in contrast, tends to have the opposite effect, and causes children to become less responsible, and more likely to blame others, and more dependent on other people, including the abusers.

The reasons for this lack of responsibility and lack of independence has to do with the way negative reinforcement affects mental development. Constantly being attacked by caregivers, peers, or other adults, repeatedly reinforces negative behaviors, like social avoidance, anger issues, low self-confidence, insecurity, or substance use to treat a mental disorder, among other developmental problems. The child, who would otherwise be a healthy, self-confident, high achieving student, may become depressed and develop anger issues. In addition to mental problems, not having a safe or stable environment in which to do homework may cause a significant decline in academic performance, or increase the preoccupation with drug use. And those problems may make the child increasingly more susceptible to personal attacks, criticism, and blame.

Preventing adverse childhood experiences from occurring in the first place would solve many problems. That requires strong parenting skills that focus on encouraging the development of abilities and skills that lead to positive outcomes. But in terms of intervention, proving child abuse maybe nearly impossible if the child does not have physical signs of abuse, or the abusers are not guilty of other criminal activities. If we lived in a society of glass houses where everyone could observe everyone else's behavior, abusers would be easy to spot. But in our society, behind closed doors and brick walls, no one really knows what goes on.

We only see what people want us to see. No person is programmed like a robot to exhibit only one type of behavior. And that includes abusers. People act differently towards different people in different circumstances, depending on mood, habits, and the nature of the relationship. So whether we perceive a person as an abuser, or monster, depends on how they behave in our company, and the person they want us to see. They may treat people who judge them, authority figures who protect them, and managers who pay their salary, differently than they treat their own children in private. People may have secret behaviors they are not willing to share, whether it is a substance use problem, child maltreatment, or some other problem.

Abusers, like all other people, want to avoid adverse judgment and may not admit to the abuse. They may instead deny the guilt, or manipulate the facts to cover up the abuse. They may put all the guilt, blame, and responsibility on the child, making the child appear to be the culprit. They may say that the reason their child has emotional problems, a substance abuse problem, or poor academic performance is not because the child is being abused, but because the child is spoiled, or is a terrible child who is genetically and mentally defective. And who are unsuspecting people supposed to believe? Should they believe the adult who goes to church, keeps a clean home, is respectable and polite, and appears to be caring for children? Or should they side with the child, who appears to have mental and behavioral problems? Even in a non-shared environment, where siblings of the same family have different experiences with the same family members, child maltreatment may not be apparent.

This creates an impossible and irresoluble problem for the child, especially if the child has mental disorders and behavioral problems resulting from the abuse and is unable to make sense out of what is happening. Children do not have the intellectual abilities, independence, or experience to confidently defend themselves when revealing unsubstantiated claims of abuse, and do not know the consequences if they tried. Children who are abused often have developmental deficiencies and may lack of confidence in their abilities. They may fear that they will not be believed, or fear injury or death from the abusive parent, or may fear some other catastrophic consequence. They depend on the support of their caregivers, who control much of their lives and how they are perceived. So it may be easier to hide the abuse, rather than take on the impossible challenge of confronting it.

Not every young person who develops an addiction, engages in criminal activities, or commits a mass shooting, has a mental disorder resulting from childhood abuse. Each person with a mental health problem is a unique case. And the behavior may be the result of the child's own choices or abnormal development.

So intervening is a problem because the doctor or specialist may be compelled to take a bias position and start accusing caregivers of abuse, or take the caregiver's side and start attacking the child. Both have the ability to manipulate the facts to get what they want. And both may be equally guilty and partly to blame. Some people may have the biased opinion that all parents are caring about the welfare of their children and would never do anything to harm them. And that may be especially true when the parents are particularly convincing, financially successful, considered to be smart people, and are not suspicious.

If people were more educated about how mental disorders result from child maltreatment and abusive relationships, they may be more likely to consider the possibility that the child may not be entirely to blame for behavioral problems. If a child has an emotional disorder, or some other mental disorder, people may have a reason to suspect child abuse, rather than simply treating the child as genetically or mentally defective. If the child is moved into a more supportive environment that provides positive reinforcement and encouragement, the child's behavior may change. Also educating people about Behavioral Science, and specifically how to improve their own mental condition and self-confidence, would help people in general with their life issues, in addition to victims who never receive help.

When young people become adults, they are legally responsible for their decisions. So if they do not learn to think independently as children, and develop a strong sense of responsibility and self-confidence, they must develop those traits as an adult or the consequence will be social problems.

7

Physical Conditioning

Conditioning is a common practice in physical health, diet, and the development of healthier habits to reduce many health related risk factors and improve health related outcomes. Improved fitness increases productivity, prolongs the amount of time you are able to work, and improves the body's ability to overcome muscle tension from daily stress. People who eat a healthier diet are able to earn more income as a result of increased energy levels, alertness, mood, increased confidence in abilities, and improved performance. Healthier people have fewer sick days, and a lower risk of developing a serious health condition that may require surgery, medication, or medical attention that would prevent them from working. Medical expenses from those conditions have the potential to drain a person's savings and leave the person financially disadvantaged later in life.

Studies show that nutrition and exercise are significant factors of brain health and brain function. Decreased brain function in areas, like the prefrontal cortex, may cause a lack of motivation, increased stress, a lack of impulse control, and poor decisions. At a TED talk, Neuroscientist Sandrine Thuret talked about neurogenesis and, specifically, the hippocampus's ability to grow new nerve cells. Her studies found that moderate engagement in stimulating activities, like learning, running, eating foods, like chocolate or blueberries, and moderate calorie restriction, helped to increase neurogenesis. Factors that decreased neurogenesis included stress, sleep deprivation, aging, excessive alcohol consumption, and others.[67]

What we eat goes into our brain and body composition. A lack of specific nutrients may cause a nutrient deficiency and injury. The sodium from highly salty foods clots blood. Fats and sugars are stored as fat. That does not mean that excluding these ingredients from a diet is healthier, but that people need to consume those ingredients with care and moderation. Some diets are better for body composition than others. In recent years, researchers found that a diet consisting of vegetables, vegetable oil, and moderate amounts of protein, a diet they called the "Mediterranean Diet," reduced the risk of death from heart disease, cancer, and reduced the risk of other adverse conditions.[50]

Alternatively, many Americans frequently consume a fast food diet that consists of highly-processed foods loaded with fats, sugars, artificial colors and flavors, and preservatives. Fast food producers are financially incentivized to reduce costs, increase shelf-life, and artificially improve flavor, rather focusing exclusively on nutrition. Fast food chains are known to increase meal portion sizes, forcing consumers to pay more for larger meals. What was the jumbo sized meal in previous decades is now a medium sized meal and costs three times as much. By increasing meal portions, fast food producers effectively double their sales and fatten their profit margins. And if people develop a habit of regularly eating fast food, and do not prepare nutritious meals that are tasty and filling, then they are not controlling their calorie intake in a way that controls their Energy Balance. In other words, they no longer balance the calories consumed with the calories used during physical activity.[12] And that exposes people to a greater risk of becoming overweight, developing type-2 diabetes, hypertension, coronary heart disease, and stroke.[12]

CHAPTER VI:
RESPONSIBILITY

People are legally responsible for their behavior when they mature in to adulthood. This presumes they understand the meaning of responsibility, are able to think independently, and use their own judgment when making decisions. In legal proceedings, lawyers sometimes rely on a Psychologist to prove, or disprove, a defendant's responsibility for committing a crime. And to avoid punishment, a defendant may try to avoid accepting responsibility for a decision that harmed another person by denying involvement or blaming other factors. In this chapter, we explore the meaning of responsibility, what defines a person's scope of responsibility, and how people become more responsible for their future when trying to create the lives they want.

1
The Meaning of Responsibility

The word responsibility has many definitions. But, from a Behavioral Science perspective, we could define it as the ability to respond to a set of circumstances. In some instances, like when a child is drowning in a swimming pool, a person may be legally required to respond. But the amount of responsibility people really have for the outcomes they live with is debatable. A person's responsibility for an outcome largely depends on whether that person is able to respond to the circumstances that created the outcome. When we have a choice about whether to take action or not, and can foresee the potential consequences, then we have some responsibility for what happens. When we are not able to respond, and do not have a choice, then we could not be responsible for the final outcome.

In our daily lives, this sense of responsibility influences behavior in very obvious and observable ways. We observe it when watching two strangers interact, or when someone tries to take care of valued possessions. This awareness of our responsibility can be exhausting if we are in a constant battle to keep up with a demanding schedule, or are constantly responding to people's demands. It always seems like we could do a little more, work a little harder, or be a little more prepared, in the process of succeeding or failing to create the outcomes we want.

Habits also have an influence on people's responsibility. A person may develop a habit of being nice to coworkers because he wants to be recognized as a kind and caring person who understands that those people do not deserve to be treated harshly. Or a person may develop a habit of automatically cleaning things and staying organized. Or a person may develop a habit of leaving things dirty, depending on that person's sense of obligation to keeping those things clean. These are all learned responses to everyday circumstances that strengthen, and become more automatic, with repetition.

At the same time, people are not responsible for everything in their lives. They do not have a choice about their genes, parents, or the environment in which they grew up. But they do have responsibility for the choices they make.

And that is true even when people are forced to make less than desirable decisions because of the limited opportunities available to them. Imagine being in a combat situation and an enemy combatant is holding a gun to your head and threatening to kill you if you do not comply. Your only choices are to follow the orders or be shot. If you are in a hostage situation and have negotiation training, you may approach the situation differently than someone who relies on instinct and intuition alone. And that training may give you more options and choices, and may help you create a more favorable outcome. Many of the circumstances in our daily lives are similar in that we have limited options to choose from. And we are forced to work with what we have or accept a less desirable outcome.

In many circumstances, people do not have a choice in matters (e.g., they may be under the control of an authority figure), and are not responsible for the final decision or its outcome. A business manager, who knows the larger strategic goals of the organization, makes choices for employees to align their efforts with organizational goals. A child may have a parent who made a choice that influenced the entire course of the child's life, either in a positive or negative way. And we rely on specialists and experts, who we believe are more knowledgeable and experienced, to make choices for us.

2

Scope of Responsibility

People are the product of their environment and the product of their own making. In the first sense, we are not responsible for everything that happens to us. We are not responsible for our genes, the identity of our parents, the political or economic conditions we were born into, the environment in which we grew up, or being harmed by environmental forces. We are not responsible for the world that created and sustains us, and serves us in so many ways. And we are not responsible for the adversity, accidents, hardship, natural disasters, and forces beyond our control. This is true, even when we do have some responsibility in serving others, taking care of the environment, and protecting each other as the law requires.

We also have cognitive limitations. We never fully know what we stand to gain or lose when making decisions. Even with the best intentions, our decisions inevitably produce unintended consequences. And not only are we unable to solve other people's problems; sometimes, we are unable to solve our own problems, especially those that are permanent and unchangeable.

Certain mental disorders develop as a result of environmental influences. For example, a person may develop Post Traumatic Stress Disorder (PTSD) as a result of combat exposure, or a person may develop an emotional disorder as a result of living in an abusive relationship. A person with an emotional disorder may develop anger issues, may violently attack the abuser, may become depressed and suicidal, or may decide to medicate the disorder with an intoxicating substance. All of these are instances in which the disorder leads to terrible choices that could lead to law enforcement intervention.

People develop habits in how they learn to respond to routine circumstances. As those responses are repeated with increasing frequency, they strengthen into conditioned responses that shape the personality. People who live in dangerous conditions, for example, learn to think protectively and defensively. Different conditions present different challenges, elicit different responses, provide different opportunities, promote different personality traits, and lead to different life-altering decisions. If life were like a card game, then you have to play with the hand you were dealt, even if you were not dealt a good hand.

But despite the fact that people are partly the product of their environment; they are also the product of their own making. The achievements that people labor over simply do not happen to them. They made those things happen as a result of their choices and hard work. We continuously make choices about how to solve our problems and have the ability to shape and influence the outcomes we live with. And we can glaringly see this causal relationship between decisions and their consequences when reflecting on decisions that led to dramatically poor outcomes. Creating the results we want is usually not the consequence of any single decision or mistake, but the sum of many choices, decisions, and mistakes, combined with favorable and unfavorable conditions, and a little perseverance.

Consider the decisions made by players in a sports event. A reporter may say that a player made a terrible decision in the final seconds of the game that cost the team victory. But, many factors actually contributed to the team's defeat, like practice, diet, exercise, and strategy. Games are sometimes won or lost before the players step onto the field. And improving performance with physical conditioning, testing abilities, reducing uncertainty, and having a little determination and persistence, influences the final result.

As a general Principle of Responsibility, we may not be entirely responsible for everything that happens to us, but we are responsible, to a limited extent, for the choices we make. And we can choose how to handle life circumstances, how to solve difficult problems, and whether to seek help. Some choices are influenced by natural instinctive reactions, like panicking and running in fear from whatever scares us, or becoming angry and violently attacking anything that threatens us. Others are learned responses that are influenced by training, like learning to relax and carefully examining the available options to determine the best course of action.

People do not always consider, or even know about, all of the options available to them when making decisions. Consider the fact that we live in a marketing environment that continuously bombards us with advertisements enticing us to consume unhealthy foods and beverages. But that marketing cannot be entirely blamed for people's poor choices or problems in communities. Advertisements do not force us to do anything. We still have a choice. And many people live in that same marketing environment and choose to avoid those foods and beverages, and live very healthy and active lives.

So, when two people grow up in the same environment and develop differently, how do their choices and environment factor into their development? Why does one child grow up in a dangerous neighborhood become a criminal, while his best friend becomes a respectable lawyer? Genes and biology play a significant part in how people behave and develop. Some people may be genetically predisposed to having characteristics that give them more or less of an advantage in some professions. But genes do not determine a person's family members, personal treatment, experiences, culture, community, prevailing beliefs, education, or guidance. And people's choices are guided by more than genes. They are guided by ideas, knowledge, the lack of knowledge, and social influences. The child who decided to become a lawyer may have found guidance from within, in terms of envisioning the life he wanted. Or maybe he had an inspirational figure in his life that helped to guide his choices. But, somehow, he became aware of options available to him that the other child did not consider, or did not pursue.

3

Obligations

People's responsibilities usually exist in the context of fulfilling some obligation, whether it is a social agreement or formal contract. People have informal obligations to family and friends. And they may have formal agreements with employers, business associates, or lenders. And when a person is needed by friends, family, or coworkers, and has a sense of obligation to help those people, it may give a person's life greater meaning and purpose. And that sense of being needed could further motivate a person to be responsible.

But what could explain why some people seem to be so much more responsible in fulfilling their obligations than others? Some people seem to have an extreme sense of devotion to their perceived obligations. They may devote their entire lives to a greater cause or purpose, like their religious beliefs or career. Or a person may risk personal safety to save another person, like when a soldier throws himself on a grenade to save his fellow soldiers, or when a fireman saves a child from a burning building. Many of these risks are, of course, occupational hazards that are part of the job. But sometimes people feel obligated to help others who are in need, even when they are not required to by explicit agreement, like when a person saves another person from being killed in a train accident. Those actions are often praised and called altruistic, or lauded as heroic.

One explanation for why some people seem to be more responsible may have to do with their motivation. They may have an interest in helping people affected by problems they experienced in their own lives, which creates a greater sense of obligation to those people. Another explanation may be habit formation and how people learn to respond to routine circumstances. Habits sometimes develop as a result of training that occurred at some point during the person's development, or from professional training later in life. If you witness an auto-pedestrian accident in which a person was seriously injured, you may call emergency services. But an off duty emergency responder, like a paramedic or police officer, may be compelled to respond as a result of having training and preparation. When a person knows how to respond to the demands presented by specific circumstances, the person's response tends to be stronger and more automatic.

People have an idea about what they are obligated to do in different circumstances. If a person feels obligated to help someone who was seriously injured in an accident and fails to do so, that person may feel a sense of guilt for neglecting to respond. If you witnessed an event in which a person was seriously injured and you did not respond, would you tell someone about it, feel guilty for neglecting to respond, or create a reason for not trying to help? Some people may not feel obligated to help at all. When a person does not have emergency services training, many professionals advise against helping as a way of preventing more injuries. So all of these different factors, including personal safety, social influences, training, and motivation may influence how people respond in fulfilling their obligations.

4

Answering for Decisions

When people show a clear lack of responsibility, how do they answer to those who are affected by it? To illustrate this idea, imagine that Fran is waiting for Brad to meet her at the coffee shop at 8am and Brad does not show up. After waiting for some time and attempting to contact him, Fran decides she may never schedule breakfast with him again unless he provides a good reason for his absence.

When people are forced to answer for their decisions, especially if they had a negative impact on someone else, they sometimes try to avoid adverse judgment and adverse treatment by providing a valid reason for their decisions. The most certain way to avoid adverse judgment is by working harder, or striving to be more dependable, when trying to fulfill obligations so that excuses are unnecessary. But doing that is not always so easy. People make mistakes and have shortcomings, and they have ulterior interests. And, sometimes, they are compelled to lie to avoid accepting responsibility for their shortcomings and mistakes, and may blame those problems on circumstances beyond their control.

This attempt to defend one's actions from accusations of negligence or wrongdoing is sometimes called a character defense, which is an attempt to protect one's interests and influence outcomes. In an earlier chapter on satisfaction, we looked at how a person's behavior is profoundly influenced by what that person stands to gain or lose. And people get very angry and dramatic when defending their actions and protecting their interests from condemning accusations because the inability to do so could lead to significant losses as a result of rejection, adverse treatment, or even worse if a crime was committed.

On an instinctive level, the display of anger is an emotional defense, the outward characteristics of which provide physical and emotional protection. Physiologist Walter Cannon once described the defense of anger as expressing itself in the bristling of hair and uncovering of teeth in rage and hostility. The "rage response" is displayed in a "crouching body," a "frowning brow," and "grinding teeth." The individual mutters "growled threats," has "tightened fists," and seizes a weapon in preparation for attack. All of these behaviors, he says, are useful in preparation for the struggle.[10]

People are usually not that dramatic when they get angry. But fear, and the desire for protection, compels people to thoughtlessly pulverize any pestilent little thing that threatens their interests, no matter how small or insignificant it is. This desire for protection is territorial, in a way, because people try to protect things that could be taken from them, like employment, an intimate relationship, or a material possession, which provokes a response to defend it, or take it back. A child may express this tendency most uninhibitedly when a toy or food is taken away, especially when the child begins to cry, kick, or scream, because someone threatens to deprive him of the thing he wants. Adults behave similarly when they throw fits, lie, or start arguments, to get what they want.

People may have good and justifiable reasons for their actions. But they also make mistakes and have errors in judgment and recollection, and are affected by unforeseen events they could never predict or prepare for. And if those people are unable to defend their actions, and show that they are dependable and can be trusted, it may mean losing a job, a friendship, or something else. The following sections look at some approaches people use to either accept, or avoid accepting, responsibility for their decisions, and how people use deception to defend and protect their interests.

5
Rationalization

When we talk about rationalization as a character defense, we are talking about an attempt to show that one's actions were based on valid and justifiable reasons to prevent a negative outcome. Eric Fromm gave an example of how the "function of rationalization" enables a person to "prove to himself and to others that his action is determined by reason, common sense, or at least conventional morality." And no matter how "unreasonable or immoral an action may be, man has an insuperable urge to rationalize it."[31] Some people seem to perceive themselves as righteous and justified in everything they do, no matter how wrongful, hurtful, or destructive they are. They want to explain their behavior, and show that their decisions are based on perfectly valid reasons.

Our natural defenses are continuously working to protect us from physical, social, and financial threats. So when a particularly bad decision results in a horrendous or devastating outcome, the people responsible may not want to accept responsibility because of the negative attribution it could ascribe to their character, which could threaten their freedom, trustworthiness, or livelihood. The easiest way to avoid accepting responsibility for an unfair loss is to either show how the act was not deliberate, or deny committing the act all together. And that defense is often used in criminal trials where the defendant either claims self-defense for a violent act, or completely denies committing the act.

Alfred Adler gave another example of a person who wanted to deny ever making mistakes and, instead, wanted to blame his parents or education for his mistakes. He complained that nobody ever cared for him and that he was mistreated. He wanted to be "excused of further responsibility" to avoid all criticism and blame. The reason he could never fulfill his life ambitions was always someone else's fault. He never changed his behavior, but "turns and twists and distorts his experiences until they fit it." Even the child, Adler said, creates excuses for his failures, claiming that he was "too weak or petted," or siblings thwarted his development.[2] Psychologists call the tendency to accept responsibility for one's successes, and blame other things and other people for their failures, a self-serving bias.[9]

The fact that our personal development is, to some extent, shaped and nurtured by other people like caregivers, educators, trainers, and managers makes it easy to pass blame onto them for our shortcomings. And despite the fact that, as adults, we are responsible for taking on more responsibility for our personal development, some people take rationalization to its furthest extent and blame anything that is larger or more powerful than themselves for the problems in their lives.

In *Totem and Taboo*, Sigmund Freud called this tendency a "delusion of persecution," in which a person's power over life-circumstances is so immensely exaggerated that every disagreeable experience falls under the responsibility of the more powerful person. He pointed out that savages blamed their kings because they had enormous power and, therefore, power over the forces of nature. This, he said, arises from the heavy burden of being dependent on someone who is more powerful, where it puts the individual in a position of blame for all misfortunes.[29]

6
Manipulation

Manipulation is a character defense that tries to alter the facts by saying anything necessary to influence an outcome. That may include saying horrible things about rivals, throwing screaming fits as children and adults sometimes do, or acting innocent around people who provide attention or money. And people who do not know what to believe may go along with it. A person who looks and sounds convincing, has a reputation of being trusted, is financially successful, and does not exhibit any indication of lying, maybe believed unconditionally.

Marketing campaigns attempt to exploit this vulnerability in human judgment. A sign in front of a restaurant may say that it is the #1 Hot Dog Restaurant in Town for 30 years, despite the fact that it is consistently rated as the worst restaurant in town. Businesses exaggerate the greatness of their products to attract customers. Similarly elected officials exaggerate their accomplishments to win voters. History tells a long story of people manipulating their way into power. And politicians will say just about anything to manipulate public perception and win an election.

Manipulation is sometimes used to influence outcomes by offensively attacking a person's character and decisions. Telling voters in an election that a rival candidate is corrupt to gain support against the person is one example. Candidates in political elections use this technique when they point out faults in their opponents, no matter how harmless or innocent those faults truly are. They label the opposition as terrible and incompetent, and create reasons for voters to dislike the opposition, to show how they are different and better.

In the words of Niccolo Machiavelli in *The Prince*, "men

judge by the eye rather than the hand, for all men can see a thing, but few come close enough to touch it. All men will see what you seem to be; only a few will know what you are, and those few will not dare to oppose the many who have the majesty of the state on their side to defend them. In all men's acts"..."it is the result that renders the verdict when there is no court of appeal."[45]

In the criminal world, the con-artist (i.e., confidence artist) exploits this weakness in judgment for the purpose committing crimes, like illicitly obtaining money or property. The con-artist lies to gain unauthorized access to information or possessions, or manipulates the facts to avoid being caught. Or an abuser may frame a victim as someone who is crazy, genetically defective, mentally unstable, mentally deficient, or as someone who cannot be believed or trusted. And by changing and altering the facts, the con-artist or abuser is able to hide that part of reality they do not want others to see.

7
Obstruction

Obstruction is a character defense that tries to cover-over and hide undesirable behaviors or character flaws that could subject a person to accusations of wrongfulness or guilt. By using this approach, the person attempts to influence outcomes by preventing people from seeing the truth. The reason we cannot always stereotype, or brand, a person as a certain type of person, is that the person in question may act differently towards different people in different circumstances, depending on the nature of their relationship. A person may have hidden behavioral patterns that one does not want specific people to see, like substance abuse or domestic abuse. And those patterns may emerge in the presence of different people in different environments. A person, who is a monster to a family member, may be the kindest and most caring person to managers and coworkers, depending on the nature of the relationship, and what they stand to gain or lose in that relationship.

Some of that tendency develops during childhood. The child wants to please the caregiver who provides food, playthings, and safety. And when the child accidentally breaks something, the child learns to hide it and act innocent to prevent the caregiver's anger and displeasure. Even as a child grows into adulthood, the child seems to gain something by hiding weaknesses, insecurities, and guilt, and using deception to avoid admitting shortcomings. People want to accept responsibility for the positive things they do, not the terrible things that subject them to condemning judgment or punishment.

People use repression to obstruct even themselves from their own problems, which can be beneficial when they fail to achieve certain goals, make mistakes, or have imperfections. Some people feel guilt and regret for their failures or inadequacies. They have sexual desires and other feelings they know is obscene and inappropriate. And by repressing those thoughts and emotions they overcome unnecessary guilt and anxiety and move on with life.

But repression also has the potential to work against the welfare of people. A person may ignore physical pain that turns out to be a cancerous tumor, or may ignore a loud bang that turns out to be a murder. When a man is perceived as someone who is trustworthy, honorable, or perhaps wealthy and well-respected, he could easily engage in improprieties and never experience negative consequences. He could continue receiving the beneficence of trust and unconditional respect because people still depend on his wealth and gifts. He becomes convinced by a lifetime of being treated well that no matter how immoral, dishonest, or corrupted he is, no matter how much his choices result in negative consequences, no matter how many people suffer at his hands, he is still convinced of his own self-righteousness. And any peccavi, any confession of guilt, may only serve to diminish him and jeopardize his interests. So he avoids admitting wrongdoing, even to himself.

8
Increasing Responsibility

When people work harder to make things happen, rather than allowing things to happen and being dissatisfied with the result, they tend to be more responsible for their lives. To illustrate this idea, imagine you purchase take-out food from a local restaurant. You get home and notice an item is wrong and a family member is upset and will not eat the food. Your first reaction may be to blame the worker who put the order together. But you also had responsibility to make sure the order was correct before leaving. You could have discovered and corrected the mistake and left with the order you paid for. You will not always be satisfied with what happens to you if you allow others to make too many decisions for you. And you will always have those people to blame for the problems you experience as a result.

All people experience failure and shortcomings in their daily lives. Maybe they are late to a meeting or forget about an appointment. But how we confront those failures, and whether we create excuses or accept responsibility for those failures, reveals how much responsibility we accept for the direction of our lives. If Bob always blames something else for his failures, and never acknowledges his part in causing them, he may never change his behavior in a way that prevents those problems from occurring in the future. But if Bob recognizes his responsibility and role in causing those failures, he may be more motivated to change the way he operates, to prevent similar failures. And that is exactly what people do when they take more responsibility for their lives: They try to recognize their responsibility for the problems in their lives and take action toward solving those problems, rather than ignoring them and allowing them to persist.

Even when people have everything they need to solve their problems, they sometimes continue to fail. Maybe they do not know how to solve their problems, or do not know what it takes to be successful. And knowing how well they are performing may be difficult if they do not receive helpful feedback. Students in school receive objective feedback when they receive grades. If a student receives a poor grade, then the student knows that more study time is required to improve performance and grades.

But even that may be subject to opinion, depending on how it is perceived. If Bob studies for an exam for twenty minutes, he may only learn about 5 topics. But in his mind, he has studied more than he has ever studied in his life and believes he will receive the highest grade on the exam. Susan, on the other hand, studies for five hours and learns about 100 topics and is still concerned about passing the exam. Obviously, Susan will receive a higher grade than Bob. And when Bob receives his grade, he may conclude that he was treated unfairly and that the instructor rigged the test against him. If Bob continues to believe that he worked hard enough and should have received a higher grade, then he will continue to fail. But if he considers the possibility that he did not work hard enough, then he may work harder the next time, and may have a better chance at passing the exam.

Outside a structured education, people do not have a way of objectively measuring their performance. So it becomes a matter of their own subjective opinion, which is heavily influenced by biases and character defenses. And that is not helpful if a person refuses to accept responsibility for a poor performance.

9

Accountability

Accountability is the ability to attribute personal responsibility to an outcome. Just as an Accountant keeps a system of ledgers to record business decisions that involve revenues and expenditures, people are able to keep a mental ledger of their own decisions, and those of other people.

And accounting for decisions that resulted in wanted gains or unwanted losses is a significant part of business management. Managers need to be able to identify decisions that harm the business, like spending millions of dollars on unnecessary services because of a lack of expertise, or losing multi-million dollar contracts because of carelessness, or making the business so inefficient that it becomes impossible to break even. Another problem is failing to adequately oversee the production of goods or services, which leads to a reduction in the quality of their products and a loss of customers.

One way to account for decisions that create wanted gains, or reduce unwanted losses, is to create an incentive system that rewards (or compensates) contributions that add value to the business, or takes corrective action for decisions that negatively impact the business. Studies have shown that by implementing an incentive system and rewarding workers for positive contributions, acknowledges the value of their hard work, and leads to improved employee satisfaction and a better retention rate. Providing rewards when workers deserve it validates their contributions and encourages employees to repeat those behaviors.[66] It also creates a sense of fairness in the work environment. If a worker is punished for doing more than what is expected, or a worker is rewarded for stealing from the business, it may lead to a perception of unfairness, dissatisfaction, and the inability to retain a talented workforce.

In the public, other types of incentive systems exist to hold people accountable for actions that have a detrimental impact on people's lives. Policy enforcement is one example that seeks to hold citizens and organizations accountable for actions that benefit or harm communities. The legal system provides services to victims of crimes to prevent perpetrators from repeating those crimes, or to help victims recover from unfair losses. And the news media can be instrumental in holding people accountable for their actions. Without a press to expose harmful activities, like businesses that dump toxic chemicals into water ways, the public may never be aware of the problem, especially if responsible parties are motivated to lie to protect their interests. And public officials may not be pressured to do anything about it.

10
Problems of Accountability

People are not always punished for decisions that cause harm and loss, and are not always credited for their hard work and contributions. When an action causes harm, citizens may employ the help of legal services to restore the damage, or to prevent the act from occurring again. But that maybe difficult if it applies to a person in a position of power. Officials, who have the authority to write the rules, may systematically exempt themselves or other people from accountability to avoid having to answer for their decisions. And that exemption may be dangerous if an official inflicts significant losses or does unnecessary harm to people.

Systematic exemption from accountability is often found in organizations where favoritism (e.g., unfair discrimination) is allowed because of cronyism, family relation, ethnic background, gender, or race. A manager may hire a friend, or return a friendly favor, by hiring someone to a management position. This creates an environment where management favors certain people over others, who may abuse their position, harm workers, or harm the business without being held accountable for their behavior.

In states, like Oklahoma, management decisions are protected by At-Will employment laws that give managers the freedom to hire, deny employment, or terminate any employee for any reason. Employees of a protected status are presumed to be protected by Federal Employment Discrimination laws. But that assumes the manager who works under the protected name of the employer always operates fairly, honestly, and with care. But if a manager is unscrupulous, then that person is in a position to abuse one's power without any accountability under civil or criminal laws.

CHAPTER VII:
STRESSORS

Stressors are experiences, events, or memories that place greater demand on a person's mental and physical resources. And stressors are inevitable as we work harder and place more demand on our own abilities to create the lives we want.

Not all stress or anger is harmful. Anger can be constructive when it motivates people to point out ongoing problems that need to be resolved, or when it motivates people to fight injustice or solve social problems. Eustress is a form of stress that is actually physically and emotionally beneficial to health. People experience eustress when they are aroused by stimulating and thrilling activities, like sports or entertainment.

But stressors also have many harmful physical and mental effects. And in this chapter, we look at those harmful effects and how to reduce them by developing healthier stress habits.

1
Health Related Outcomes

If we look at the biology of the stress response, we would see how fears and worries increase heart rate and breathing, and mobilize the body for action, all of which place greater demand on the body's internal systems to work harder and move faster. The nervous system discharges hormones from the endocrine glands, including the hypothalamus, adrenal, and pituitary glands, which are responsible for survival instincts, sexual behaviors, emotions, alertness, excitement, aggression, and metabolism. That causes the secretion of cortisol, a hormone believed to be most responsible for stress. After a distressing episode, the body activates the parasympathetic nervous system to restore homeostasis and stabilize bodily functions, and return the body back to its normal stress levels.

Chronic stress, or frequent distress caused by anything from work related demands, to crime, mental disorders, and other stress-related factors, causes a number of health related problems. Chronic stress may cause finger biting, emotional instability, altered eating and sleeping patterns, the use of alcohol or other drugs among some people, and law enforcement intervention.[16] A mental disorder can cause chronic stress as a result of remembering adverse experiences that provoke extreme anger or sadness. Those emotional and behavioral problems may cause problems in relationships, employment, and productivity.

Chronic stress also causes psychosomatic disorders, which are physical illnesses caused by alterations in biological function, body chemistry, immune suppression disease, and other diseases. Stress causes muscle tension, increases heart rate and blood pressure, blood sugar rises, blood is directed away from the gut where it is normally needed for digestion, and it clots more easily. The American Institute of Stress says that chronic stress may lead to hypertension, heart attacks, strokes, diabetes, and other problems.[6]

Most people experience a major stressor at some point in life, like a traumatic event that causes a major life change. Extremely stressful events, like experiencing a natural catastrophe or combat, may have a lasting impact on a person. And those events are known to cause mental disorders, like Post-traumatic Stress Disorder (PTSD), that leave a residue of physiological damage, memories, and emotions that remain with the person long after the event.

In 2006, the Hurricane Katrina Community Advisory Group released a survey of 1,043 adults who lived through hurricane Katrina in August of 2005, one of the most costly and deadly storms in United States history to strike the coast of Alabama, Mississippi, and Louisiana. According to the report, almost all of the participants "reported experiencing at least one significant hurricane-related stressor, such as the death of a loved one, a major financial loss, extreme physical adversity, and extreme psychological adversity."[37]

Despite an increased prevalence of mental problems after the hurricane, the desire to commit suicide among the general population did not increase. Interviewees seemed optimistic about rebuilding their lives. The majority of them said the hurricane gave their lives greater purpose and helped them to get in touch with their "inner strengths."[37] People affected by the hurricane faced greater physical and financial insecurity after the storm. But the way they chose to handle that stress improved their outlook on life. Having discovered these newfound inner strengths allowed them to overcome the new problems they faced. And more than 89 percent of the respondents said that their ability to cope with future distress improved.[37]

2
Biological Influences

Biological conditions have an influence on the amount of stress people experience each day. Stress levels tend to increase or decrease when people experience pain, sleepiness, hunger, pleasure, and comfort. Years ago, Bronwyn Fryer wrote an article in the Harvard Business Review about how excessive sleepiness impairs response time, memory, attention span, cognitive performance, judgment, and problem solving. According to the article, sleepiness may be the reason for close to one-fifth of motor vehicle accidents in the United States. Dr. Charles Czeisler, who was interviewed in the article, described the affects of sleep deprivation as being similar to "legal drunkenness" and may be considered a "health hazard" among workers.[32] Excessive sleepiness, in addition to alcohol, and other adverse conditions, causes people to make poor decisions that result in unintended consequences, which further increases stress levels.

Some parts of the brain are more influential on decisions than others. The hypothalamus, which is part of the limbic system in the central core of the central nervous system, is believed to be responsible for much of human motivation like fear, emotional behavior, sleep, appetite, and sexuality. This instinctual part of the brain ensures survival, and compels people in the human world to seek safety in social and financial security. During a moment of panic, the hypothalamus sends a signal to the autonomic nervous system to increase heart rate, breathing, and blood flow, to prepare the body for action. Other biological systems that alert us about threats to our wellbeing, like fear, hunger, or pain, further compel behavior and have a powerful influence on decisions.

In addition to these instinctual parts of the brain are those that enable us to make rational decisions, like the prefrontal cortex, which slowly develops as young people grow into adulthood and continue to age. The prefrontal cortex is believed to be responsible for complex planning, strategy, problem solving, social behavior, and goal oriented behavior. An underdeveloped, or low functioning, prefrontal cortex is sometimes attributed to poor judgment and risky behavior. A significant decline in brain function, or brain damage, in the prefrontal cortex may cause a lack of motivation, poor decisions, or exhibiting inappropriate social behaviors.

In a story on National Public Radio, Laurence Steinberg who does Functional Magnetic Resonance Imaging (or fMRI) research, said that young people sometimes make terrible decisions because their judgment is influenced more by hormones and peer pressure when they are in the company of peers. These are instances in which adolescents are trying to act in their best interest, but sometimes make poor decisions instead. Neuroscientist B. J. Casey, who was featured in the story, likened the prefrontal cortex to the logical and rational Mr. Spock from the 1960's television show Star Trek, while the limbic system is more like the emotional and impulsive Captain Kirk. The Captain is always looking out for threats and rewards, but always needs Mr. Spock to restrain his decisions with logic and reason.[68] Adolescents do not always have this logic and reason restraining their behavior in the company of peers. So they uninhibitedly fight threats and pursue rewards, sometimes resulting in poor decisions.

While this tendency is perceived to be more common among adolescents; it happens to adults as well. The limbic system (i.e., the survival part of the brain) is always influencing our decisions, and sometimes more than the prefrontal cortex (i.e., the rational part of the brain). The excitement an adult experiences as a result of stress, anger, fear, or sexual arousal, has a powerful influence on behavior. And when people face the prospect of severe loss or harm, they sometimes make impulsive and irrational decisions out of desperation to prevent a negative outcome. In other words, the limbic system, which is supposed to be responsible for human survival and reproduction, sometimes causes people to make very stupid decisions if not kept in check by a healthy and active prefrontal cortex.

3
The Fear Response

Fear, and anything that evokes fear, is a common stressor. Suppose we have a vested interest in finishing a project on time and within budget. But when time constraints begin to work against our interests, it evokes fear and distress, and may spur us to work faster, concentrate harder, and work longer hours to complete the project. Similarly, we experience stress as we strive to achieve goals, keep appointments, satisfy the demands of employers and clients, and create the outcomes we want.

Fear is one of the more powerful, compelling, and ubiquitous influences on behavior. We can observe fear when a person moves slightly faster to avoid being late to an appointment, or when a person recoils after hearing a loud and disturbing sound. When faced with circumstances that illicit fear, we have a few choices: We could escape the threat, combat the threat, or play dead. This is known as the fight-or-flight response, which influences how we choose to engage or avoid the challenges presented by circumstances. The most extreme and exaggerated forms of the fight-or-flight response are murder and suicide. A person may commit murder to annihilate a perceive threat. Or a person may commit suicide in flight from the stresses, burdens, and hardships of living. But people also develop many subtle habits in response to circumstances that illicit fear as we see in personal relationships when a person develops a habit of conflict or avoidance with certain people.

Research by Psychologists Daniel Kahneman and Amos Tversky found that people tend to be loss averse, and go to extra effort to avoid loss. And the innate, instinctive, influence of fear may explain why. People sometimes take on increasingly greater risks, like continuing to gamble away their life savings while believing that they will get it back to avoid a loss. Or a motorist will speed down the interstate, putting other driver's lives at risk to avoid being late for work. Intuitively this makes sense because the prospect of losing something we want, not only evokes the fear of losing it, but provokes the defenses needed to protect it.

So, fear has the potential to work for us or work against us. Fear works for us when it keeps us safe, helps us to assess when situations are too risky, and compels us to behave responsibly. Fear about potential future outcomes (i.e., destitution, poverty, or loneliness), compels people to be productive, develop skills, seek employment, and develop beneficial relationships. People go to extra effort to avoid negatively impacting people who depend on them, who may criticize them, blame them, or accuse them of wrongdoing. In many ways, fear about future outcomes motivates people to be more responsible and dependable, and enables them to make decisions that prevent loss and hardship.

But fear also works against people. Social anxiety may prevent a person from talking to people and forming beneficial relationships. Or fears of small creatures, heights, or the fear of failure, may prevent a person from pursuing beneficial opportunities. Getting into the habit of overreacting in overly fearful ways by retreating from the problems of living, or by responding with extreme aggression to everyday circumstances, not only causes social problems, it is harmful because it works against a person's wellbeing and that of other people. These are instances in which the stress caused by fear results in harmful and sometimes deadly consequences.

4
Stress Response Habits

In the chapter on judgment, we looked at how, when faced with decisions that are risky or impact people's lives, a person may make better decisions by suspending judgment until enough information is available to be certain about the decision. The problem is: People are emotional. And people are instinctively inclined to respond to immediate conditions, like hunger, emotions, or tiredness. Judgment under stress tends to be impaired by impulsivity, fears, and intuition that override deliberate reason. Being in a state of anger, rage, or extreme fear, may cause a person to make an impulsive fight-or-flight decision that has an unintended long-term consequence. Even when people are well aware of those problems, they may continue to have stress management and anger management problems.

The reason for this apparent lack of self-control is that people are continuously confronted with, and responding to, circumstances beyond their control. And those circumstances present challenges, like dangers, frustrating obstacles, and preventable errors. And it's easy to blame, and become angry and frustrated with, those external forces. Minor stressors, like waiting in line at the supermarket, or getting stuck in traffic, may suddenly become a major stressor if the person increasingly continues to focus blame, anger, and aggression on those things.

If being late to work threatens Bob's employment, then being late to work is certainly a fear reinforced by real consequences. But overreacting to those fears and desperately speeding to work on the interstate, becoming frustrated, angry, and hostile towards slow drivers, tends to work against people's safety and welfare. The driver risks getting into an accident, and endangers the lives of other motorists because of poor planning and desperation. That is why stress, according to the American Institute of Stress, causes crime, violence, unhealthy behaviors, and loneliness, and is responsible for the majority of visits to primary care physicians.[5]

Different types of stressors influence judgment differently. A person who is physically fit and ready to take-on the challenge of loading boxes onto trucks at a distribution center may not consider the job a problem. But John, who has back pain, may consider the same job too stressful and, therefore, may be at long-term risk of physical injury. This could influence John's decision to suddenly quit, refuse to do his job, or ignore the problem only to have it develop into a serious and debilitating medical condition. The choices he makes will ultimately have an impact on his long-term wellbeing as a result of the outcomes he will be forced to live with.

Much of that stress can be managed by creating positive stress habits, and learning new ways of responding to stressful episodes. Responding with anger towards slow traffic will not help you get to your destination any sooner. And, instead, it could cause you to get into an accident if you begin making impulsive, emotion fueled, decisions. Rather than focusing blame and anger on forces beyond your control, recognize your own role and responsibility in creating those circumstances, and refocus energy on solving the problem. Some possible solutions may be to pull over and find an alternate route, or give yourself more time the next time you travel.

Another example of a positive stress habit is learning to relax and stay calm long before emotions begin to develop. Staying relaxed in otherwise stressful, or nerve racking, circumstances helps a person to maintain self-control and make deliberate decisions by not allowing emotions to influence decisions. Learning to relax emotionally, even in high performance scenarios, is a learned response that may improve with practice.

Another positive stress habit involves changing your state of mind by changing your activities and environment. Consider one of my colleges (we will call him Jerry) a software engineer who spends most of his work day writing and debugging code. One day, he pounded on his desk and exclaimed: "What is wrong with this stupid thing!" He pounded keys on his keyboard, made frustrated grunts, and uttered annoyed remarks. Clearly, Jerry was trying to fix a bug in a program, but did not know what was causing it. He thought the program should work, but for some unknown reason it did not.

Jerry's stress and frustration will probably slow him down as he throws fits and breaks things. He has attached a negative emotion to it, called it a piece of crap, and is now attacking the problem in all the wrong ways, which will not help him to solve the problem any quicker. After noticing Jerry's frustration, I asked him to join me for a game of Table Tennis in the recreation room. After we played a few sets, our spirits were lifted and Jerry was in high spirits and smiling. Within a couple of minutes after returning, he exclaimed "Yes, I figured it out!"

Walking away from a stressful problem before it becomes too emotional prevents a negative stress response. Changing your state of mind by engaging in different activities and changing what you are experiencing helps to break negative emotional habits that would lead to unwanted outcomes. This is not necessarily the same as mentally going to our happy place. It is an act of physically changing your environment and engaging in different activities that stimulate different emotions, evoke different responses, and create different memories.

People also use other techniques to change their state of mind and train their brain to relax. Some people use meditation or mindfulness to develop impulse control and focus on something, like breathing, to clear the restless mind of residual emotions, achieve peace of mind, and become more in tune with the moment. Finding time away from work related responsibilities for leisure, games, creative activities, or recreation may influence your emotional disposition, improve your sense of wellbeing, and create positive memories. Stress management experts also suggest managing your time more effectively. Plan things out in advance to prevent unnecessary distress caused by being late for deadlines, appointments, or work. Create realistic expectations, get enough sleep, develop satisfying relationships, and avoid too much confrontation and argument.[49]

Management may also be able to do things to improve morale and reduce stress in the work environment, which could further improve worker productivity and organizational performance. When workers receive more for their labor than a paycheck, in terms of positive experiences, opportunities to learn and develop, and receive credit for their hard work and sacrifices, they may be more satisfied with their job, more interested in contributing to the organization, and being more productive and helpful as coworkers.

CHAPTER VIII:
MENTAL DISORDERS

Mental health is not necessarily attributed to the absence of mental disorders. In fact, a person could have one or more mental disorders and have no symptom of a mental health problem. And, in this chapter, we look at the differences between the two and the possibility of preventing or reducing certain disorders that have the potential to cause social problems, like substance abuse, physical abuse, crime, or poverty.

Many mental disorders result from genetic, neurological, biochemical, or anatomical abnormalities and are not preventable. But in earlier chapter on conditioning, we looked at how some disorders have environmental origins and are preventable, or at least may be mitigated. For example, we looked at how prolonged exposure to the conditions of combat may lead to Post Traumatic Stress Disorder, or how an abusive relationship may lead to an emotional disorder. In this chapter, we look at some different types of mental disorders and their influence on mental health, and how to improve mental health by applying the concepts in this book.

1

Relationships & Mental Health

Many mental health experts today often recommend developing closer personal relationships as a way of improving mental health. In 2010, Debra Umberson and Jennifer Montez at the University of Texas at Austin published a paper that compiled evidence from numerous studies showing the affects of social isolation and relationships. They pointed out that social isolation is sometimes used by captors to torture prisoners. Their report does not go into detail about how the imprisonment, and what their captors did to them, affected the prisoners mentally or emotionally. But they show that social isolation among the public, leads to a greater likelihood of health problems and death. Social support, in contrast, reduces stress, improves wellbeing, and provides other mental health benefits.[69] So what is the actual role of relationships, if any, in reducing or mitigating mental health problems?

In our private lives, we may intuitively observe how personal relationships are mentally and socially reinforcing. Social interaction provides a sense of wellbeing, a sense of identity, and a sense that everything will be fine. And having obligations to friends, family, or employers may even give life greater meaning and purpose, and a greater need to be responsible in fulfilling those obligations.

But the notion that the closeness of personal relationships determines personal happiness, or mental health, has many contradictions. People who are socially isolated, or are not in a close relationship with other people, do not, by some law of nature, succumb to madness, become angry with the world, or go insane. Many people live very lonely and solitary lives, whether they choose to or not. And that fact, alone, does not mean they have mental health problems or are deprived of wellbeing. Even when a person is lonely, that person has choices, some control over life, and the ability to make responsible decisions.

Consider the 17th century Physicist and Mathematician Isaac Newton who was known to live a very solitary life, never married or had many friends, and was known to go into periods of seclusion. Aside from brief periods of mental instability, he was mostly healthy and lived to the age of 84. Inventor Nikola Tesla, famed for making contributions to AC power, the modern power grid, X-ray technology, Radar, remote control, and other technologies, was very reclusive, never had any known relationships, and was very healthy and lived to the age of 86. So people who are socially isolated are fully capable of behaving responsibly, even when they do not have the same obligations as people in close personal relationships.

Another problem is that certain people seem to have loving families, many friends and, in some cases, successful careers as corporate executives or entrepreneurs, and end up killing themselves or other people. Many corporate executive suicides, like Enron executive J. Clifford Baxter, happen after accusations of scandal and legal problems, and may be attributed to the impending legal consequences. But during July of 2013, Swisscom CEO Carsten Schloter, and weeks later Zurich Insurance Group CFO Pierre Wauthier, both committed suicide and the incidences were attributed to stress and demanding work schedules.[7]

The reasons for these suicides are uncertain. A common presumption is that corporate executives were not hired to their positions because they had noticeable mental health problems or significant character flaws, but because they were dependable and trustworthy people. But corporate executives are often exposed to significant stressors. When a business question arises that management cannot answer, especially when those questions have significant legal or financial ramifications, that question is usually directed to upper management. And the burden of responding to everyone's demands and making the right decisions makes for a very demanding and stressful schedule.

The news media also associates loneliness and social isolation to mental health problems. When a mass-shooting occurs, a key piece of information reported is that the perpetrator was lonely and antisocial. And that isolation likely contributed to plotting an attack in secrecy and killing in large numbers. But we know that logic does not apply to all mass-shootings. And every day, a local news station reports about person who murders a spouse or commits murder-suicide. These incidences are more common and involve people who have friends and family. The only difference is that those crimes are not as shocking because of the number of deaths involved.

Certainly, many complex biological, chemical, and environmental influences are responsible for violent behaviors and mental health problems. So solving those problems is usually more complex than any simplistic solution, like medication or relationships. Many personal relationships are even harmful, especially abusive relationships. So social engagement and personal relationships may improve a person's sense of wellbeing, in most circumstances. But many other factors, like mental disorders, have a much greater influence on a person's mental health.

2
Mental Disorders

A mental disorder is a mental condition that significantly impairs a person's self-control, judgment, and decisions. The Department of Health and Human Services has defined mental disorders as "health conditions that are characterized by alterations in thinking, mood, or behavior (or some combination thereof), which are associated with distress and/or impaired functioning and spawn a host of human problems that may include disability, pain, or death." People do not have a choice about whether they have a mental disorder any more than they have a choice about having a physical illness or a disease. So learning to recognize mental disorders may not only help those who have them, it could help people, like family members, managers, or coworkers to recognize and interpret those disorders.

Mental disorders are not the same as mental illnesses, and do not necessarily prevent people from pursuing life goals or creating positive outcomes. Mental disorders do not include common stressors, religious rituals, socially accepted religious beliefs, social deviance, societal conflicts, or cultural conflicts. But a mental condition that causes a person to be inconsolably sad for unknown reasons, or a mental condition that causes a person to be extremely hostile for unknown reasons, may be a mental disorder.

The most common mental disorders are anxiety disorders, which, according to the United States Department of Health and Human Services, are known to affect nearly one out of four people in the United States in a given year.[19] A few of those include phobias, mood disorders, panic disorder, obsessive compulsive disorder, social anxiety disorder, generalized anxiety disorder, or posttraumatic stress disorder. A person with a panic disorder may experience brief moments of fear frequently throughout the day. These conditions are typically harmless and very common, and usually do not prevent people from being productive, engaging in healthy relationships, or discharging emotions in socially responsible ways.

If we compared a phobia to a physical illness, it would be comparable to an allergy. Having a fear of heights, dark places, spiders, snakes, small spaces, isolation, or loneliness is like being allergic to those things. And those fears are rational, to some extent, because it is true that a person could fall to one's death, get bit by an insect and get sick, or drowned in water. Those tendencies are part of how people protect themselves from the dangers of living to ensure their survival.

Mental health and wellness is not necessarily attributed

to the absence of phobias, mental allergens, or other mild mental disorders that are common among people. Severe mental disorders, on the other hand, may prevent a person from functioning normally and may cause mental and physical health problems. A person with a severe mental disorder may not make decisions that are in one's best interests, and instead may make decisions that lead to hospitalization, incarceration, or homelessness. A mental disorder that is severe enough to threaten a person (e.g., suicidal tendencies), or other people (e.g. homicidal tendencies), is characteristic of a mental illness.

A mass shooter who acts alone most likely has a severe mental disorder that developed into a mental health problem. The shooter, in question, may be angry at the world and may have disorderly, erratic, and emotionally charged hostility directed towards people in general. In these circumstances, the victims may not know the perpetrator, and obviously did not do anything to provoke the attack. The behavior is purely the result of a mental condition and is, therefore, indicative of a mental health problem.

Not all mental health problems are so obvious. Some people have a severe mental disorder and seem perfectly rational and may have many friends, a loyal family, and a successful career. And we will briefly look at some of those disorders and how they affect people's lives later in this chapter.

3
The Cost of Mental Disorders

A study by the United States Department of Health and Human Services found that "mental and behavioral disorders and serious emotional disturbances (SEDs) in children and adolescents can lead to school failure, alcohol or illicit drug use, violence, or suicide." Among people age 65 and older, an estimated 25 percent, or "(8.6 million) experience specific mental disorders, such as depression, anxiety, substance abuse, and dementia, that are not part of normal aging." Only 2.6 to 2.8 percent of adults in the United States suffer from the most severe and debilitating disorders. And the majority of people with mental disorders neglect to seek help.

The HHS study found that untreated mental disorders cost in terms of "lost productivity due to illness, premature death, criminal justice interaction process, and property loss." During 1996, almost $70 billion was spent in the United States treating and diagnosing mental disorders. Nearly $75 billion more was spent on disability insurance and lost productivity because of illness or deaths that were attributed to mental disorders. And another $6 billion was spent on property loss, law enforcement, and criminal justice because of mental disorders that same year.[19] All of these problems impact the lives of people who create them, and the families, employers, law enforcement officers, victims, and community collectively.

4

Depression

In one year, depression cost the United States $40 billion due to lost productivity and health care costs, according to a Department of Health and Human Services report, making it a "leading cause of absenteeism and diminished productivity" in the workplace.[19] People are more likely to experience depression when they are distressed, pessimistic, have a low self-worth, or have a medical condition, like cancer, stroke, or a hormonal disorder. Extreme life changes requiring significant adjustment, like unemployment, as well as financial problems, problematic relationships, and significant losses, are also causes of depression.[53]

A person who is in good mental condition may perceive oneself as having enough control over life circumstances to overcome life challenges, and have a sense that everything will be fine. But people who are depressed, in contrast, may perceive a lack of control over life, and feel helplessness to do anything about it. Psychologist Martin Seligman called this condition learned helplessness. And during the 1960's at the University of Pennsylvania, Seligman and Steven Maier did some experimental research to collect evidence for learned helplessness.

In their experiment, they created two groups of dogs: An escape group and a no-escape group. The escape group consisted of dogs that were exposed to electric shocks, which they had the option of terminating by pressing a panel. The no-escape group consisted of dogs that were exposed to electric shocks they were not able to escape, or control in any way. When a dog from the escape group was put into a shuttle box, which is a large box divided into two compartments, and electric current was supplied to the floor of the dog's compartment, the dog jumped over the dividing partition into the other compartment to escape the shock. But when dogs from the no-escape group were put into the shuttle box and were exposed to an electric shock, they did not try to escape, even when escape was possible.

The conclusion that Seligman and Maier arrived at was that, because the dogs in the escape group learned their actions could stop the electric shocks, they learned to take action and jump into the other compartment. And because the dogs in the no-escape group learned that their actions could not stop the electric shocks, they did not try and developed learned helplessness. Seligman later suggested that this could explain depression in people.[36]

The extent to which learned helplessness develops in people is unknown. A person who is in an abusive relationship, like a child who is unable to escape the daily maltreatment of an abusive parent, may develop learned helplessness. Or anyone trapped in miserable and impoverished circumstances may be more susceptible to a sense of helplessness. Learning to tolerate, accept, and live with misery, certainly has an influence a person's emotional wellbeing and outlook on life. A person with learned helplessness may be able to overcome the condition by learning new skills, improving confidence in certain abilities, and improving one's abilities to overcome life challenges, as we have seen in earlier chapters. All of these provide a greater sense of control over the direction of one's life, and an improved outlook.

5
Schizophrenia

Schizophrenia influences judgment, decisions, and life outcomes as a result of altered cognitive processes, perceptions, speech, and emotions. The disorder is rare and is known to affect about one percent of the population in the United States. Those who suffer hear voices, hallucinate, and have false beliefs, and other symptoms that come and go. At times an affected person may see, smell, or feel things that are not present, like the nervous system is sending false signals to the brain.

Symptoms include delusions that others are trying to control one's thoughts through brain or radio waves, or periods of disorganized thinking where a person's speech has no logical meaning, or the individual has a hard time completing sentences, or makes up words. People with schizophrenia often have problems with memory, attention span, personal hygiene, and making decisions based on facts. All of these make it difficult to earn a living and have normal relationships. Studies show that people with schizophrenia are more likely to attempt suicide. And about 10 percent of those that try actually succeed.[54]

6
Substance Use Disorder

Substance use disorder, or substance abuse, is a mental

disorder characterized by the uncontrollable consumption of an intoxicating substance that leads to a variety of health, legal, and financial problems. The root causes of substance abuse are complex because the person may be trying to medicate an emotional disorder, like excessive anger or sadness, or a chemical dependence.

People who consume substances recreationally usually set rules for their consumption, maybe having one or two alcoholic beverages in an hour to entertain, so they do not consume too much. But a person with a substance use disorder may continue to drink uncontrollably, or may develop regular habits of substance use, in ways that cause a variety of harmful side-effects. The most detrimental of those side effects are behavioral problems and impaired thinking, which causes other preventable problems. And just like other habits, substance use habits may be very difficult to break if the user develops a dependency, and the habit is hardwired into the brain and influences decisions in a more automatic way.

In recent years, addiction researchers found that eight to ten percent of people over the age of eleven have a substance addiction, costing the United States about $700 billion as a result of law enforcement intervention, missed work, or health care costs. The study published in the New England Journal of Medicine by Nora Volkow, George Koob, and A. Thomas McLellan collected data about substance addiction in the United States to better understand the addiction cycle. For simplicity, their research divided the substance dependence cycle into three stages: 1) binging and intoxication; 2) withdrawal and negative affects; and 3) preoccupation and anticipation.

In the first stage, the user views the experience produced by binging and intoxication as a reward. And the greater the perceived reward, the greater number of harmful consequences the user is willing to tolerate to engage in the activity. When the user is no longer intoxicated, the user experiences withdrawal and the negative affect stage of the addiction cycle. Since prolonged substance use interferes with brain chemistry, during the withdrawal stage dopamine levels are decreased, reward circuits are desensitized, and stress reactions grow stronger. In the last stage of the cycle, these changes in brain chemistry and brain function cause the user to become preoccupied with, and anticipate, the consumption of the substance. And despite the potential for terrible and devastating consequences, or the desire to quit, the user develops a substance dependence.[74]

When a user is trapped in the addiction cycle, the person not only anticipates the pleasure of intoxication, but the negative effects of not using it. The user begins to depend on the substance to avoid withdrawal symptoms that may include tiredness, fatigue, absent mindedness, or could be as severe as hallucinations and seizures, depending on the substance.[27] The withdrawal symptoms become a source of worry and anxiety, and not using it creates a perception of insecurity and risk. If the user develops a tolerance for the drug, dosage must be increased to achieve the same effect. And that increase in dosage has the potential to become dangerous and life-threatening, or lead to mental damage and dysfunction.

Excessive substance use also has side effects that interfere with responsibilities and personal relationships. Those side effects may alter a person's behavior, physical appearance, speech, memory, performance, and ability to fulfill obligations. The prolonged effects of intoxication may lead to social avoidance, the inability to perform work related responsibilities, and a decline in self-confidence, all of which makes a person more vulnerable to verbal attacks and criticism and leads to defensiveness, insecurity, and a sense of constantly being under attack. The U.S. Department of Health and Human Services says that impaired thinking caused by substance use leads to drownings, crimes, imprisonment, and death, and leads to hospital bills from emergency room visits, long-term healthcare costs, and rehabilitation costs.[20]

Ending an addiction cycle may require help from professional services to quickly accelerate the resolution of addiction problems before they become severe. Some of that may involve treating underlying triggers of addition, like stress or an emotional disorder. People with addictions may receive long-term help by joining a support group where members understand the problems of addiction and are willing to provide assistance.

7

Recognizing a Mental Health Problem

A person with a mild mental disorder, like a phobia, or anxiety disorder, is not mentally ill and may live a very healthy and productive life. But a person with a severe mental disorder that threatens the person's wellbeing, or that of other people, is symptomatic of a mental health problem.

When we look at how mental health is defined by the U.S. Department of Health and Human Services, and how healthy people "cope with the stresses of life" and are able to "be productive," we could see how not being able to do those things could threaten a person's livelihood. A severe mental disorder, like severe depression, may prevent a person from being emotionally stable enough, or emotionally positive enough, to engage in normal daily activities.

A study by the Department of Health and Human Services concluded that during the year 2000 about 90 percent of all suicides were due to mental disorders, substance abuse, or a combination of both.[19] Studies by the National Center for Injury Prevention and Control identified some risk factors for suicide, which include substance abuse, hopelessness, impulsivity, substantial social or economic losses, and physical illness.[52] Their studies also suggest that the reason young people feel the need to commit suicide is that they are overwhelmed by stress and depression and find suicide to be a solution to their problems. And in 2001, people over the age of 65 who committed suicide were diagnosed with moderate depression, a physical illness, or were divorced or widowed.[52]

People with one or more mental disorders usually live their entire lives without hurting themselves or other people. But if a disorder continues to get worse, and anger or hostility continues to escalate into violent behaviors, it could result in imprisonment or death. Homicides due to mental health problems are commonly perpetrated against family members, such as a spouse or a child. The question is: At what point does an enraged person go from screaming, throwing things, slamming doors, and having anger issues, to picking up a weapon and committing murder as a result of a mental health problem?

CHAPTER IX:
SOCIAL SKILLS

In an earlier chapter on motivation, we looked at how people are motivated to pursue their private interests. That is, they tend to give more attention to their own interests, which includes their finances, family, or property. Those pursuits limit the amount of help and attention they give other people, and the amount of help and attention they receive in return. But people are also motivated to cooperate and help each other because pursuing certain types of interests, like earning an income, having a loving relationship, in addition to the pursuit of many other interests, all depend on personal relationships. And this chapter looks at the role of social skills in creating those relationships.

In Dale Carnegie's book *How to Win Friends & Influence People*, he wrote in great length about how people are absorbed in themselves and their own interests. And if you want to make friends, according to Carnegie, you need to be interested in them, listen to them, and focus on their lives, rather than trying to make them interested in you. If you avoid criticizing people, he emphasized, and recognize that they and their lives are important, you not only act in their interests, they are more likely to value your opinion and consider you a friend.[11]

1
Strengthening Relationships

One of the more powerful social skills is being able to strengthen relationships, or prevent them from falling apart. Some people are better at it than others. The ability to develop and strengthen relationships partly depends on time spent together engaging in positive and beneficial activities. That, by itself, can be challenging since people spend much of their time pursuing their own private interests.

The way you make people feel, and the emotions they attribute to you, influences how they interact with you, and their sense of obligation to you. Emotions are strongly influenced by the amount of support or conflict people receive. People tend to think favorably and inclusively towards those who support their ideas and act in their interests. And they think unfavorably, defensively, and exclusively towards those who conflict with, or act against, their interests.

2
Dependability

The ability to depend on a person to perform a role, whether that involves being a friend, coworker, or business partner, depends on two things. The first is that the person is not actively working against you, or your interests, which we could call the trust factor. The second involves the person's ability to perform the role, which we could call the confidence factor.

The first of these (i.e., the trust factor), tends to strengthen personal relationships, teamwork, and cooperation. In 2012, the internet search engine company Google conducted an internal study, called Project Aristotle, that sought to research the factors that make the most productive and creative teams. They found that despite the differences in personality types among team members, the most productive teams allowed members to take risks in meetings without subjecting them to feelings of negative judgment for their ideas or suggestions.[23]

Teamwork requires trust and the ability of team members to depend on each other for support. When team members attack each other, or their ideas, they may attribute negative emotions and negative labels to one another, which could further cause a lack of cooperation and an unwillingness to give input or make an effort. Being positive and receptive to each other's ideas and avoiding negative criticism gives those involved the opportunity to influence the outcome in a way that satisfies everyone. And just as trust applies to teamwork, it applies to other types of personal relationships, like friendships, intimate partnerships, and families.

Even in an intimate relationship, the role of the intimate partner, according to Abraham Maslow, is to allow the partner to "open up," to "drop his defenses," to "let himself be naked not only physically but psychologically and spiritually as well."[47] Sigmund Freud wrote about how this sense of security provides the loved one with freedom from criticism, where one is valued more than others, something he called "sexual overvaluation."[30] This trust allows people to express their deeper sexuality and interests without feeling threatened.

The second factor (i.e., the confidence factor), refers to our confidence in a person's ability to perform a role. That tends to be gained or lost depending on personal history. People are often credited for their successes and blamed for their failures. And people are especially credited for failures that leave others with negative experiences that caused harm or loss. People tend to gain other people's confidence when they appear to be successful and lose confidence when they continue to fail.

Many employers run background checks to make sure they can have confidence in an applicant when making a hiring decision. Lenders may check the financial history of loan applicants to make sure they have proven reliability to repay the loan. But confidence, or the lack thereof, is not always permanent and unchangeable. People do have the ability to develop new skills, and shape and influence the trust and confidence of people. And the next section looks at how to do that with strong communication skills.

3

Communication Skills

Communication skills are techniques for effectively conveying and exchanging information. And they are a significant part of building cooperative relationships and working towards common interests. We may not have control over other people's behavior. But we are able to influence them, change how they perceive us, and build trust and confidence when trying to strengthen relationships.

In business, communication may consist of marketing to potential buyers, or communication between management and workers. A lack of clear communication between any of these parties causes failure in business operations and prevents management from identifying and solving problems. And those failures may lead to a decline in customer satisfaction and revenue, or a decline in worker satisfaction and productivity.

Effective communication is both a skill of conveying information and a skill of listening. When we factor in other forms of communication, like non-verbal communication (e.g., symbols), verbal communication, or visual communication (e.g., body language), any one of these may be ambiguous and misunderstood, and may lead to errors and mistakes. People are able to improve their non-verbal skills, like sending and receiving social signals, or reading social cues, starting conversations, and avoiding people who are not socially engaged. But to be truly effective at communication, you need to reduce uncertainty and ambiguity in the meaning of communication by providing more information, asking questions, learning to be receptive, and listening, which reduces mistakes and misunderstandings. All of these are habits that may be improved by testing your ability to convey information and listen to feedback.

4

Conflict Resolution Skills

In previous chapters, we looked at some reasons why personal conflicts occur. People may have different, conflicting, interests. They may have problems of self-control, problems managing stress, or mental disorders that influence their behavior. If we do not see these within ourselves, we see them in our coworkers, managers, or in family members. And many of those problems may be mitigated with conflict resolution skills.

Conflict occurs when a person's interests are under attack, or threatened, by other people. This is especially true when people are on opposing sides of an argument. And a common response is to protect and defend those interests, usually by avoiding the conflict, or by counterattacking. Conflict may become mutually reinforcing if those involved begin openly attacking one another with emotionally provocative insensitive remarks, or impulsive acts, that cause emotions to escalate.

Georg Simmel once described what he called the deep hatred that grows out of "broken love," how it "splits the security and unity of our self-conception" so that we "unavoidably make the object of this intolerable feeling pay for it. We cover our secret awareness of our own responsibility for it by hatred which makes it easy for us to pass all responsibility on to the other."[61] Resolving a conflict can be expensive if it requires hiring an intermediary, like a counselor or attorney, which is an expense that could be avoided by developing more effective conflict resolution skills.

Our ability to resolve conflict largely depends on how we approach conflict. In the minds of people, perception is truth. If you disagree with a person and attempt to change that person's opinion by arguing a conflicting view point, you may instead escalate the disagreement into a verbal conflict. Rather than impetuously counter-attacking and inflaming disagreements into full-fledged conflicts, a more constructive approach may be to ask questions and listen, and try to understand the other person's perspective. Or when conflict begins to develop, which can cause those involved to make terrible decisions, you could walk away and allow the person to have those feelings, and figure out a different way to approach the problem. If you have the slightest uncertainty in your argument, especially if you are not an expert on the subject, then using good judgment and doing research to verify the accuracy of your argument helps to avoid unnecessary conflict.

Most things are not worth arguing over. And winning an argument is not the same as creating the best outcome for everyone. Rather than perpetuating senseless conflict, focus on what you are really trying to accomplish and on the outcome you are trying to create. People are much more willing to cooperate and make everyone better off if they do not feel that they, or their ideas, are under attack.

The most effective tactic to resolving any type of conflict is to do whatever necessary to get everyone involved on the same side, even if that means getting on the side of your enemy. This tactic may prove to be effective in even the most difficult to resolve conflicts that continue to be perpetually inflamed by hatred, intolerance, and violence that impoverishes families and makes their lives miserable. If those involved were on the same side in the real war against the violence and hatred that destroys so many lives and families, and were more outspoken in getting other people to join, they could possibly work together to build a safer and more prosperous future.

5
Ending Harmful Relationships

Ending a harmful relationship is social skill that is necessary for preventing problems, like feelings of being victimized, the development of mental disorders, or violent attacks that may be perpetrated by the abuser or against the abuser to stop the abuse. People have different approaches to dealing with these circumstances depending on how severe the treatment is, and whether it consists of verbal attacks that are emotionally abusive, or physical assault.

Emotionally provocative attacks that occur daily for a prolonged period of time, perpetuate and strengthen social responses of avoidance or counter-attacks. If an abuser is able to recognize the behavior as causing harm, and can recognize the verbal attacks as a habit that should be ended, that person may be able to change, to some extent. But the potential for change also depends on whether a person's behavior is influenced by a mental disorder, and whether that person has concern for the welfare and well-being of other people.

Most people know that it's wrong to capriciously attack another person, threaten a person with excessive malice, or make a person suffer. And sometimes an abuser will accept responsibility for the behavior when it is exposed and becomes obvious to other people. But when that does not happen, the abuser has a choice about whether to accept responsibility for acts that are wrong and condemning. And the abuser may, instead, choose to manipulate the facts to make it appear that one's actions were justifiable by blaming the person being abused, and having no guilt or remorse for the behavior.

People who are heavily invested in a relationship because they are partners in marriage or business may have the most difficulty ending the relationship. A married person with children who seeks a divorce may lose a substantial amount of social and financial support if finding a new partner is difficult. That person may lose a house, a standard of living, the ability to finance a child's education, part of one's social identity, and potentially a retirement.

The unfortunate reality is that, because ending a close partnership may be more difficult and devastating than living in it, people often end those relationships only when circumstances are so extreme, and emotions are so inflamed, that they are hostile toward each other. If that relationship does end, the ability to treat each other fairly, and start over without feeling victimized, is essential to the wellbeing of everyone involved. That may involve forming an agreement at the beginning of the relationship to help each other in the event the relationship ends.

CHAPTER X:
SOCIAL RESPONSIBILITY

Social responsibility refers to the impact that decisions have on people's public lives, their community, and the environment. That impact may be a wanted benefit or unwanted harm or loss. Different forms of social responsibility permeate throughout our lives in many unexpected ways, even in areas where Science has traditionally struggled. When we look at art, love, or spirituality, each has some impact on people (even if it is emotional impact) and, therefore, ascribes attribution and responsibility to the creator. Guiding principles, like the Golden Rule, and treating people the way we like to be treated, promotes socially responsible behavior. Some political movements, like the Civil Rights movement, influenced the creation of socially responsible policies to reduce unfair losses to affected groups of people.

In business, social responsibility is called Corporate Social Responsibility and focuses on reducing the detrimental impact that business operations have on people or the environment. Consider the fact that businesses often use plastics and other packaging materials to lower the cost of producing and shipping goods. Consumers buy those goods and discard the one-time-use packaging as waste that ends up in landfills, or pollutes the environment. In economic terms, that pollution is considered to be a negative externality, which is something from a producer's activities that society agrees to pay part of the cost for. A business may strive to be more socially responsible by trying to reduce negative externalities. They may create policies and programs that strive to reduce carbon emissions or reduce the possibility of exposing the public, workers, and wildlife to unsafe conditions. Some government policies may try to incentivize businesses and organizations to be more socially responsible by imposing fines for operations that have a negative impact on citizens the environment.

This chapter primarily focuses on Political Social Responsibility and the social and financial impact of governmental policies and programs on citizens and businesses. That involves looking at whether enforcing certain policies, or implementing certain programs, places excessive burdens or excessive costs on government organizations, citizens, and whether government officials are doing too much or not enough. And knowing that usually requires more than an intuitive hunch, or a gut instinct.

1

Social Problems

Just as people have the freedom to manage their lives as they choose in pursuit of their private interests, they are not forced to behave responsibly, or consider how their decisions impact people or the environment. People do not always see the incentive of behaving responsibly if they can get ahead by taking from others, or are able to obtain what they want by endangering the public or the environment. And the result is social problems, which includes anything that harms people, or is a burden to the public, including crime, personal mistreatment, mass-shootings, pollution and other problems that compel government officials to spend billions of dollars on programs designed to mitigate the impact of those problems on communities.

When we look at people from every demographic of society, we find people who have life goals for their finances, family, and retirement. And people usually do not have a reason to commit a crime. But a percentage of those people will engage in activities that expose them to the risk of incarceration where they would be deprived, or prevented, from obtaining those things.

The root causes of criminal behaviors are complex and unique to each case. They may be attributed to carelessness, domestic abuse, mental disorders, substance abuse, a lack of educational opportunities, economic conditions, or a lack of intervention. People who experience social problems may be exclusively responsible, or may have physical or mental disabilities, mental disorders, or mental health problems. And because of that complexity, preventing all social problems is not possible.

But public officials are able to make measurable progress at improving the living conditions and quality of life. They are able to create policies and programs that provide citizens with more opportunities for improved health, safety, and employment. And the way they do that is by providing public goods and services.

2
Public Goods & Services

People have different opinions about the role of government in their lives. And those differences influence their political affiliation. But whatever those opinions are, most people agree that the role of government is to provide public goods or services, which consist of things that private entities, like private citizens and private businesses, are unable to provide for themselves, like infrastructure and protection. Local governments may provide public services, like police and fire departments, or public goods, like building and repairing local roads. And the federal government may provide national defense, and interstate infrastructure, for private businesses to transport materials for the construction of housing, manufacturing facilities, and office buildings, .so they can produce and distribute private goods and services. And many of these government products are financed by taxpayer revenue or government issued bonds. Consequently, taxpayers tend to be more or less satisfied with the public goods and services they receive. And having access to services that protect citizens, and ensure fair, safe, and healthy living conditions gives citizens fewer reasons to be discontented with their government.

At one time in the United States, the supply and demand of labor determined the price of labor in the same way that market forces determine the price of other goods and services. When that happens, as the supply of labor increases, the hourly price of labor decreases. At some point, it decreases below a living wage, assuming a 40 hour work week, a point at which workers are unable to afford basic living expenses. And that creates two potential economic consequences. Workers earning below a subsistence wage do not have the discretionary income to contribute to the growth of the economy. And, secondly, people become more reliant on public assistance and may be motivated to commit crimes to obtain basic necessities.

3
Influences on Policy

Getting more of what we want as citizens is not the same as creating the best outcomes for society. If everyone got what they wanted from Government, and government spending was not narrowly focused to serve the best interests of greater society, it would bankrupt the State. And that is one of the problems many democracies face as state and national debts continue to climb and states file for bankruptcy. But not all democracies are on the verge of bankruptcy. Many are very financially strong and have a strong infrastructure. The reasons for those differences may have more to do with the way government resources are managed, the strength of local economies, and what influences policy and program decisions.

Policy decisions have many influences. Ideally elected officials are influenced by the public interests of citizens and businesses, and the desire for better government provided goods and services. They may listen to experts and scientists about the impact of an action, or inaction, on a community. But they are also influenced by their own private interests, beliefs, and political affiliations, and make decisions that make them, their family, their business, or financial donors better off. Officials, like all other people, make decisions about how to solve problems based on intuition and biases and are influenced by the opinions and biases of lobbyists, interest groups, and voters. And while many of those decisions benefit the public, officials also make decisions that have unintended consequences and do unnecessary harm. An official may neglect to provide adequate services, or fail to protect citizens, or may create an unnecessary program that is too costly and provides little or no benefit. Often, what seemed like a good idea, may have turned out to be a terrible idea.

Examples of government mistakes are easy to find in just about any part of the world. In 2014, officials in Flint, Michigan, switched the city's water supply to a different water source, contaminating the drinking water with high levels of lead and other heavy metals that caused serious health problems among residents. In 2007, the I-35W Bridge over the Mississippi river in Minnesota suddenly collapsed, killing 13 people and injuring more than 140. And we could certainly make an intuitive judgment about the safety of a water source, or the safety of a bridge; but knowing whether they will actually have a negative impact on the community requires more than an optimistic and hopeful belief.

4
Approaches to Mitigating Social Problems

The criminal justice system is operated by people who, like the rest of us, make decisions based on intuitive judgments. And those intuitive decisions sometimes create problems. An offender who victimizes another person may receive no punishment. Innocent people are sometimes convicted of crimes they did not commit. Or a person convicted of a victimless Misdemeanor crime may spend more years in prison than someone convicted of a violent Felony. People may also be reluctant to do anything about those problems because they are especially biased against criminal offenders and tend to avoid helping them.

The goal of policy enforcement is to incentivize people to comply with the law because it provides, what some Economists call, a Penalty Avoidance Benefit, which is the benefit an entity, such as a person or business, receives from operating in accordance with laws and regulations.[58] These may include money, freedom, additional liberties, additional protections, and certain advantages in the marketplace where a criminal record would put a person at a disadvantage. Violating legal prohibitions makes a person more vulnerable to fines, prosecution, and incarceration, and the offender may be subject to greater intolerance and discrimination, depending on the nature of the crime.

Another goal of policy enforcement is to make sure citizens are safe from harm and unfair losses by fining motorists for speeding, or jailing people who steal or commit violent assault. These actions are necessary to keep citizens safe. But they rarely do anything to solve the behavioral and social problems that caused the criminal offense in the first place. Some correctional facilities provide programs to rehabilitate offenders. But they may be ineffective and produce inconsistent results. And many prisoners who are released, re-offend, and the problem remains or grows worse.

In recent decades, the prevailing attitude among many officials in the United States is to make the labeling and incarceration more severe and to build more prisons, despite having some of the highest incarceration rates in the world. Politicians seeking reelection have tried to appeal to voter biases by enacting get-tough-on-crime laws and mandatory sentencing laws that require people who are repeat offenders of Misdemeanor crimes to be labeled a Felon and, in some cases, be required to spend years in prison.

Part of the problem with increasing punishments is that policy makers may never see, or fully understand, the social and economic consequences of their actions, or how they impact the lives of citizens and their families. If they are biased, they may not even care about the consequences of their actions, until they are forced to face the reality of prison overcrowding, or an overwhelmed criminal justice system that jails innocent people, or frees offenders, because it is incapable of processing all of the offenses.

Misdemeanor crimes are considered minor petty offenses punishable by fines instead of incarceration. Felonies are more severe crimes that may be punishable by incarceration lasting for more than one year, or punishable by death. In addition to fines or incarceration, Felons may lose a number of rights as citizens, such as the right to serve on a jury, the right to own a fire arm, the right to vote, and the right to practice certain professions. The practice of labeling a person a Felon for a Misdemeanor crime has a number of costs to the offender and the community.

Consider in 1995, shortly after the State of California enacted a three-strikes law, a man was sentenced to 25-years to life for stealing a slice of pizza from some children. Officials in California later recognized those laws as extreme and revised them to include only violent offenders. But more recently in 2016, a man was arrested in Louisiana for stealing about $30 worth of candy bars. In Louisiana, which has one of the highest incarceration rates in the world, having more than two convictions for shoplifting is a felony. And because he had prior non-violent felony convictions for shoplifting, he faced 20 years to life. In those cases, the District Attorney has some say in the defendant's charges. But once the defendant is charged, the judge presiding over the case has little discretion in changing the punishment because of mandatory sentencing laws. The cost of incarceration to the State of Louisiana, at the time, was about $18,000 per year and about $360,000 over a 20-year period, to imprison someone for stealing about $30 worth of candy bars.[3]

The punishment of alcohol related traffic violations is another example of a Misdemeanor crime punishable by a fine, or temporary loss of driving privileges, and a criminal record that may be expunged after a few years. But in many states, offenders who have repeat offenses within a certain period of time, are labeled Felons for life.

Those laws come with a cost to communities and their economies in the long-term. But to understand that cost, we need to look at what citizens stand to gain or lose in the process, starting with policies that have a substantial financial impact to private citizens, and a substantial cost to communities. If taxpayers spend an increasing amount of money incarcerating people, they forgo the opportunity to finance other public goods, like education, public safety, or public infrastructure, which may help to reduce crime and improve social conditions. That money could be spent removing urban decay, like abandon buildings that may be occupied by vagrants or criminals. It could be spent improving urban life and creating programs that give young people opportunities to develop skills and have positive experiences.

Imposing harsher punishments on misdemeanor crimes also impacts families, and may cause further social and economic losses by removing a productive taxpayer from the community. Even if a person has a perfect record afterword, receives an advanced level of education, makes all the right choices, and contributes to the greater good, a person convicted of a Felony for a victimless Misdemeanor offense remains a Felon. Ten or twenty years after the fact, if the person seeks a Pardon for the Felony, that person goes through the same process as a capital offender (i.e., someone who is guilty for a crime, like murder), which is a process designed to hear from the victims. And that person will likely be denied the pardon, even for a victimless Misdemeanor crime. That denial would do nothing to keep citizens safer, or warn citizens of a potential danger, or prevent the person from reoffending. It simply subjects the person to greater discrimination and potential difficulty finding employment, and would force the person to live with unnecessary hardship.

Felons tend to be portrayed in television dramas, movies, and the news as hardened career criminals that victimize people and should never be given a second chance. And that may be the mental image most average people have of Felons, without any distinction between a Capital Offense, like murder, and a Misdemeanor crime, like a victimless traffic ticket. In minds of law abiding citizens, a Felon is a Felon. And that criminal history will likely influence a hiring manager's decision about whether to hire an applicant.

Companies today usually require applicants to specify on the application whether they have ever been convicted of a Misdemeanor or Felony. And even when applicants are not required to do that, those records may be freely available on a State website. Hiring managers could, then, screen candidates based on those facts without even looking at the nature of the offense or when it occurred.

Sociology Professor Devah Pager conducted a study in 2001, that showed people who were formerly incarcerated as having a lower position in firms and making less income. A number of theories exist for this, she says: "the labeling effects of criminal stigma, the disruption of social and family networks, the loss of human capital, institutional trauma, and legal barriers to employment."[55] One problem, she says, is that a criminal record attaches a kind of "negative credential" that may qualify a person for exclusion in the employment process.

To observe this, Pager conducted a study with two black, and two white, male college students that were described as "bright and articulate." Together, they audited a total of 350 employers in Milwaukee, Wisconsin, a State where people with a criminal record are protected by law from being discriminated against by employers, unless the offense is relevant to the position. The students were randomly assigned a criminal record of having a felony conviction during different weeks, which consisted of "possession of cocaine with intent to distribute." Each applicant applied for a job requiring no more than a high school education. Under their work experience, each put work experience from the correctional facility, and each cited their parole officer as a reference on the application. About 75 percent of the employers asked the applicants about their criminal offenses and for details about those offenses. And a little more than 25 percent told the applicant they would perform a background check. Among equally qualified participants, about half as many whites with a criminal record were called back by employers in comparison with those that did not. And only one-third of the blacks with a record were called back.[55]

Pager's study shows that employment discrimination occurs even in states, like Wisconsin, that have employment protection laws. But in States, like Oklahoma, citizens are not protected by similar laws. Instead, they have At-Will employment laws that give employers the ability to hire and fire anyone they want, for any reason. Depending on the biases and opinions of hiring managers, even when a person has an advanced degree, that person may lose employment opportunities to a person with no degree because of a victimless crime committed decades prior. And that discredits the person who made substantial sacrifices and financial investment in one's education for the development of skills and human capital. And it disadvantages employers who do not recruit the brightest talent, and clients who do not receive the best service.

5

A Different Approach

An arrest is an opportunity to punish the offender and prevent additional harm by removing the offender from the community. But many officials believe that increasing the severity of punishments, with three-strikes laws, get-tough-on-crime laws, or mandatory sentencing laws, will decrease crime by deterring people from committing crimes. Those laws tend to be motivated by political biases, public outcry, news publicity, anger and the desire for revenge, and maybe the desire to appeal to voter biases.

But that does nothing to treat the actual underlying causes of crime, which may have more to do with mental disorders, a lack of education, or some other developmental problem that needs to be addressed to mitigate those problems. Instead, it imposes a disproportionate and inappropriate punishment, often for a victimless misdemeanor crime, that does excessive and unnecessary harm to people and their families. Any arrest, especially for a victimless misdemeanor crime, could also be an opportunity to correct the behavior that caused the crime, and potentially reduce the costs of treatment, mitigate social problems, and actually improve public safety in the long-term.

Offenders, today, even with lengthy prison sentences, are usually released back into the community, and into a much harsher reality than they faced before their arrest. And the question officials have to answer is: What will those inmates contribute to the community? Will they reduce social problems, influence and harm innocent citizens, or support criminal enterprises? Will they be more likely to cope with the problems they face, which may include employment discrimination and other forms of discrimination? Will their mental health, self-confidence, and outlook on life improve to the point to where they are stable and independent enough to not reoffend? It's difficult to see how any of the behavioral problems that lead to incarceration in the first place will improve while incarcerated without a program capable of improving the behaviors that enable people to be independent and responsible adults.

When a person commits a crime, like theft, or has a substance abuse problem that leads to unemployed and dependence on welfare services, mitigating that problem usually involves placing the person in a public institution, like a correctional facility or mental health facility. Both of those approaches house people differently, and treat people differently. And in terms of a criminal offense, the arrest does not consider the contributing factors that lead to the crime. And, in fact, many inmates in prison are there because of an untreated mental disorder that may require mental health services.

Correctional facilities, as their name implies, should correct an offender's behavior and prevent the person from reoffending, even if that means providing the person with some type of help. The person should at least be provided with information about personal rights and the rehabilitation process. And the treatment should be proportional to the behavior. That includes addressing incidences caused by substance abuse, and treating the substance abuse immediately after the incident.

Some things that could make a difference include improving accommodations for well behaved inmates, monitoring progress, and enrolling inmates in treatment programs. Providing access to automated learning materials, like videos and audio books, tailored to treat specific causes of behavior, could provide more treatment time, lower treatment costs, and provide more effective treatment programs.

Inmates should not receive special privileges, like access to higher education. But they should have access to education that reduces the desire to reoffend. Those programs may focus on the negative impact of the offenses, or increasing the incentive and desire to live as responsible, independent, and law abiding citizens. Testing and developing those programs may take years. But they would enable researchers to compare their results and recidivism rates, with that of existing prisons and mental health facilities.

Adam Foss, a prosecutor in Boston, gave a TED Talk about one of his cases involving a young man just out of high school who was going to be convicted of 30 Felonies for stealing 30 laptops. Instead of convicting the young man, Adam chose to help him by making sure he returned the laptops and repaid the rest of the money. The young man did community service work and was able to get a loan and go to college. Six years later, he had a degree and was a manager at a large bank. Adam's work not only saved the young man from a future incarceration and stigma where it would be difficult to find a job, it helped to change a person's life and made the community safer in the end.[28]

REFERENCES

1.   ABC News. (n.d.). More Americans Waiting Longer to Marry. ABC News. Retrieved September 12, 2015, from http://abcnews.go.com/WNT/story?id=130884&page=1

2.   Adler, A. (1949). Understanding Human Nature. (W. B. Wolfe, M.D., Trans.). (pp. 8, 134). New York: Permabooks. (Original work published 1927)

3.   All Things Considered. (April 4, 2016). New Orleans Man Faces 20 Years To Life For Candy Bar Theft. Retrieve April 5, 2016 from http://www.npr.org/2016/04/04/473004950/new-orleans-man-faces-20-years-to-life-for-candy-bar-theft

4.   American Humane. (n.d.). Emotional Abuse. Retrieved April 8, 2007, from http://www.americanhumane.org

5.   American Institute of Stress. (n.d.). Job Stress. Retrieved March 31, 2007, from http://www.stress.org/job.htm

6.   American Institute of Stress. (n.d.). Stress, Definition of Stress, Stressor, What is Stress?, Eustress?. Retrieved March 31, 2007, from http://www.stress.org/americas.htm

7.   Ansink J. (September 10, 2013). C-suite suicides: When exec life becomes a nightmare. Fortune. Retrieved September 7, 2015 from http://fortune.com/2013/09/10/c-suite-suicides-when-exec-life-becomes-a-nightmare

8.   Bergland, C. (November 20, 2013). The Size and Connectivity of the Amygdala Predicts Anxiety. Psychology Today. Retrieved October 3, 2016, from https://www.psychologytoday.com/blog/the-athletes-way/201311/the-size-and-connectivity-the-amygdala-predicts-anxiety

9. Boyes, A. (January 9, 2013). The Self-Serving Bias - Definition, Research, and Antidotes. Psychology Today. Retrieved April 24, 2016 from https://www.psychologytoday.com/blog/in-practice/201301/the-self-serving-bias-definition-research-and-antidotes

10. Cannon, W. B. (1963). Bodily Changes in Pain, Hunger, Fear and Rage. (2nd ed., pp. 195, 243-244). New York: Harper Torchbooks. (Original work published 1920)

11. Carnegie, D. (September 2, 1981). How to Win Friends & Influence People. Simon & Schuster. Rev Sub edition.

12. Centers for Disease Control and Prevention (CDC). (2006, August 26). Nutrition for Every-one. Retrieve March 30, 2007, from http://www.cdc.gov/nccdphp/dnpa/nutrition/nutrition_for_everyone/index.htm

13. Centers for Disease Control and Prevention (CDC). (2006, May 2). Fetal Alcohol Information. Retrieved April 8, 2007, from http://www.cdc.gov/ncbddd/fas/fasask.htm

14. Centre for Bhutan Studies & GNH Research. (November 2015). Bhutan's 2015 Gross National Happiness Index. Retrieved April 16, 2016 from http://www.grossnationalhappiness.com/SurveyFindings/Summaryof2015GNHIndex.pdf

15. Chompoo. (June 6, 2015). Life Satisfaction and Its 7 Contributors. Positive Psychology Program. Retrieved April 2, 2016 from https://positivepsychologyprogram.com/life-satisfaction

16. Corbin, C. B., Corbin, W. R., Welk, G. J., & Welk, K.A. (2006). Concepts of Fitness and Wellness: A Comprehensive Lifestyle Approach (6th ed., p. 295). University of Central Oklahoma. Boston: McGraw-Hill Custom Publishing.

17. Department of Health and Human Services. (2000, November). Healthy People 2010: Under-standing and Improving Health (2nd ed), pp. 9-3, 9-5, 9-6. Washington, DC: U.S. Government Printing Office.

18. Department of Health and Human Services. (2000, November). Healthy People 2010: Under-standing and Improving Health (2nd ed), pp. 16-3, 16-4, 16-5. Washington, DC: U.S. Government Printing Office.

19. Department of Health and Human Services. (2000, November). Healthy People 2010: Understanding and Improving Health (2nd ed), pp. 18-3 – 18-5, 18-15, 18-19, 18-20, 18-26. Washington, DC: U.S. Government Printing Office.

20. Department of Health and Human Services. (2000, November). Healthy People 2010: Understanding and Improving Health (2nd ed), p. 26-3. Washington, DC: U.S. Government Printing Office.

21. Diener E., Chan M. (January 11, 2011). Happy People Live Longer: Subjective Well-Being Contributes to Health and Longevity.

REFERENCES

Applied Psychology: Health and Well-Being. Retrieved April 2, 2016 from http://onlinelibrary.wiley.com/doi/10.1111/j.1758-0854.2010.01045.x/abstract

22. Doidge, N. (December 18, 2007). The Brain That Changes Itself. Penguin Books.

23. Duhigg, C. (February 25, 2016). What Google Learned From Its Quest to Build the Perfect Team. The New York Times. Retrieved April 17, 2016 from http://www.nytimes.com/2016/02/28/magazine/what-google-learned-from-its-quest-to-build-the-perfect-team.html.

24. Duhigg, C. (February 28, 2012). The Power of Habit: Why We Do What We Do in Life and Business. Random House.

25. Duhigg, C. (March 8, 2016). Smarter Faster Better: The Secrets of Being Productive in Life and Business. Random House.

26. Durkheim, Emile. Moral Education. Trans. Everett K Wilson, Herman Schnurer. New York: The Free Press of Glencoe, 1961. p. 121

27. eMedicineHealth. (2005, August 10). Substance Abuse. Retrieved March 31, 2007, from http://www.emedicinehealth.com/substance_abuse/article_em.htm

28. Foss, Adam. (February 2016). A prosecutor's vision for a better justice system. TED. Retrieved March 26, 2016, from https://www.ted.com/talks/adam_foss_a_prosecutor_s_vision_for_a_better_justice_system

29. Freud, S. (1950). Totem and Taboo. (J. Strachey, Trans.). (Standard ed., p. 63). New York: Norton. (Original work published 1913)

30. Freud, Sigmund. (1959). Group Psychology and the Analysis of the Ego. Standard ed. Trans. James Strachey. (p. 56). New York: Norton.

31. Fromm, E. (1990). The Sane Society. (p. 65). New York: Owl Books. (Original work published 1955)

32. Fryer. B., (October 2006). Sleep Deficit: The Performance Killer. Harvard Business Review. Retrieved September 13, 2015, from https://hbr.org/2006/10/sleep-deficit-the-performance-killer

33. Griffiths, A. (December 12, 2012). How the UK Police Interview Suspects. Innocence Project. Retrieved September 2, 2016 from http://www.innocenceproject.org/how-the-uk-police-interview-suspects.

34. Hock, Roger R. (2002). Forty Studies that Changed Psychology: Explorations into the History of Psychological Research 4th ed. (p. 93). Upper Saddle River, New Jersey: Prentice Hall.

35. Hock, Roger R. (2002). Forty Studies that Changed Psychology: Explorations into the History of Psychological Research. 4th ed. (pp. 71-72). Upper Saddle River, New Jersey: Prentice Hall.

36. Hock, Roger R. (2002). Forty Studies that Changed Psychology: Explorations into the History of Psychological Research. 4th ed. Upper Saddle River, New Jersey: Prentice Hall.

37. Hurricane Katrina Community Advisory Group. (2006, August 29). Overview of Baseline Survey Results: Hurricane Katrina Community Advisory Group (pp. iii, iv, 17-18, 21). Retrieved August 29, 2006 from www.hurricanekatrina.med.harvard.edu

38. Innocense Project. (n.d.). False Confessions or Admissions. Retrieved September 2, 2016 from http://www.innocenceproject.org/causes/false-confessions-admissions

39. Investopedia. (n.d.). Gambler's Fallacy. Retrieved March 19, 2016 from http://www.investopedia.com/terms/g/gamblersfallacy.asp

40. Kahneman, D. (2011). Thinking Fast and Slow. Farrar, Straus and Giroux. New York.

41. Kahneman, D. (2011). Thinking Fast and Slow. Farrar, Straus and Giroux. New York. Chapter 10.

42. Konnikova, M. (November 18, 2013). On the Face of It: The Psychology of Electability. The New Yorker. Retrieved April 17, 2016, from http://www.newyorker.com/tech/elements/on-the-face-of-it-the-psychology-of-electability

43. Landau, E. (February 10, 2009). Study: Experiences make us happier than possessions. CNN. Retrieved April 23, 2016 from http://www.cnn.com/2009/HEALTH/02/10/happiness.possessions

44. Luscombe, B. (September 6, 2010). Do We Need $75,000 a Year to Be Happy? Time. Retrieved April 17, 2016 from http://content.time.com/time/magazine/article/0,9171,2019628,00.html

45. Machiavelli, N. (1966). The Prince. (D. Donno, Trans.). (p. 70). New York: Bantam Dell. (Original work published 1532)

46. March of Dimes Foundation. (2006, April). Birth Defects. Retrieved April 8, 2007, from http://www.marchofdimes.com/professionals/14332_1206.asp

47. Maslow, A. H. (1976). The Farther Reaches of Human Nature. (p. 17). New York: Penguin.

48. Maslow, A. H. (1976). The Farther Reaches of Human Nature. (pp. 26, 117). New York: Penguin.

49. Mayo Clinic. (2006, June 26). Tips for Coping with Stress. Retrieved March 30, 2007, from http://www.mayoclinic.com/health/coping-with-stress

50. Mayo Clinic. (June 14, 2013). "Mediterranean diet: A heart-healthy eating plan" Mayo Clinic. Retrieved October 4, 2015 from http://www.mayoclinic.org/healthy-lifestyle/nutrition-and-healthy-eating/in-depth/mediterranean-diet/art-20047801

REFERENCES

51. Morin, A. (APR 9, 2015). How To Foster Good Mental Health In The Workplace. Forbes. Retrieve April 16, 2016 from http://www.forbes.com/sites/amymorin/2015/04/09/how-to-foster-good-mental-health-in-the-workplace/#6c29329925cc

52. National Center for Injury Prevention and Control. (2006, September 7). Suicide: Fact Sheet. Retrieved March 31, 2007, from http://www.cdc.gov/ncipc/factsheets/suifacts.htm

53. National Institute of Mental Health (NIMH). (2006, September 13). Depression. Retrieved March 31, 2007, from http://www.nimh.nih.gov/publicat/depression.cfm

54. National Institute of Mental Health (NIMH). (2007, January 24). Schizophrenia. Retrieved March 31, 2007, from http://www.nimh.nih.gov/publicat/schizoph.cfm

55. Pager, D. (2004). The Mark of a Criminal Record. Focus (Vol. 23, No. 2), p. 44. Retrieved April 7, 2007, from http://www.irp.wisc.edu/publications/focus/pdfs/foc232i.pdf

56. Pew Research Center. (October 30, 2014). People in Emerging Markets Catch Up to Advanced Economies in Life Satisfaction: Asians Most Optimistic about Future, Middle Easterners the Least. Retrieved April 3, 2016 from http://www.pewglobal.org/2014/10/30/people-in-emerging-markets-catch-up-to-advanced-economies-in-life-satisfaction

57. Pink, D. (April 5, 2011). Drive: The Surprising Truth About What Motivates Us. Riverhead Books.

58. Reed, W. & Schanzenbach, M. (1996). Chapter 27: OSHA - We're From the Government and We're Here to Help You. Prices and Information: A Simple Framework for Understanding Economics. Retrieved April 1, 2007, from http://www.ou.edu/class/econ3003/book/area1c27.html

59. Roediger, H. L. III, Butler, A. C. (January 2011). The critical role of retrieval practice in long-term retention. Trends in Cognitive Sciences. Retrieved March 20 2016 from http://psych.wustl.edu/memory/Roddy%20article%20PDF's/Roediger%20&%20Butler%20%282011%29_TCS.pdf

60. Shackman, G., Liu, Y., & Wang, X. (2005, Autumn). Measuring Quality of Life Using Free and Public Domain Data. Social Research Update (Issue 47). University of Surrey, Department of Sociology. Retrieved November 30, 2008, from http://sru.soc.surrey.ac.uk/SRU47.html

61. Simmel, Georg. (1955). Conflict, The Web of Group-Affiliations. Trans. Kurt H. Wolff. (p. 46). Glencoe, Illinois: The Free Press.

62. Skinner, B. F. (1976). About Behaviorism. (p. 64). New York: Vintage.

63. Skinner, B. F. (1976). About Behaviorism. (p. 70). New York: Vintage.

64. Starecheski, L. (MARCH 02, 2015). NPR. Take The ACE Quiz — And Learn What It Does And Doesn't Mean. Retrieved March 12, 2015 from http://www.npr.org/blogs/health/2015/03/02/387007941/take-the-ace-quiz-and-learn-what-it-does-and-doesnt-mean

65. Thaler, R., Sunstein, C. (February 24, 2009). Nudge: Improving Decisions About Health, Wealth, and Happiness. Penguin Books.

66. The Muse. (March 19, 2013). The Secret to Motivating Your Team. Forbes. Retrieve April 16, 2016 from http://www.forbes.com/sites/dailymuse/2013/03/19/the-secret-to-motivating-your-team/#597d4255433f

67. Thuret, S. (October 2015). You can grow new brain cells. Here's how. TED. Retrieved October 10, 2015 from https://www.ted.com/talks/sandrine_thuret_you_can_grow_new_brain_cells_here_s_how/transcript?language=en

68. Turner, C. (MARCH 11, 2015). The Teenage Brain: Spock Vs. Captain Kirk. Retrieved March 12, 2015, from http://www.npr.org/blogs/ed/2015/03/11/391864852/the-teenage-brain-spock-vs-captain-kirk

69. Umberson, D., Montez, J. K. (2010) Social Relationships and Health: A Flashpoint for Health Policy. Journal of Health and Social Behavior. Retrieved September 7, 2015 from http://hsb.sagepub.com/content/51/1_suppl/S54.full.pdf

70. Veenhoven, R. (1996). The Study of Life Satsifaction. Erasmus University Rotterdam. Retrieved April 2, 2016 from http://www2.eur.nl/fsw/research/veenhoven/Pub1990s/96d-full.pdf, p. 4

71. Veenhoven, R. (1996). The Study of Life Satsifaction. Erasmus University Rotterdam. Retrieved April 2, 2016 from http://www2.eur.nl/fsw/research/veenhoven/Pub1990s/96d-full.pdf, p. 16

72. Veenhoven, R. (1996). The Study of Life Satsifaction. Erasmus University Rotterdam. Retrieved April 2, 2016 from http://www2.eur.nl/fsw/research/veenhoven/Pub1990s/96d-full.pdf, p. 3

73. Visser, S. (June 12, 2016). Euro 2016: Dozens injured as crowds of rival fans brawl. CNN. Retrieved June 12, 2016 from http://www.cnn.com/2016/06/11/world/euro-2016-england-russia-brawl

74. Volkow, N. D., Koob, G. F., & McLellan, A. T. (January 28, 2016). Neurobiologic Advances from the Brain Disease Model of Addiction. The New England Journal of Medicine. Retrieved January 30, 2016 from http://www.nejm.org/doi/full/10.1056/NEJMra1511480

REFERENCES

75. Watson, J. B., & Rayner, R. (1920). Conditioned emotional responses. Journal of Experimental Psychology, 3.

INDEX

accountability, pp. 92-93
    public policy, p. 93
    systematically exempt, p. 93
addiction, risk of p. 13
Adler, Alfred
    confidence p. 62
    excuses, p. 86
adversity, agents of pp. 67-73
anger management, p. 102
anger
    benefits of, p. 95
    expression of, p. 84
answering for decisions, pp. 83-85
anxiety disorders, defined, p. 110
At-Will laws, pp. 94, 136
autonomic nervous system, p. 99
Bandura, Albert, Social Learning Theory, p. 66
Baxter, J. Clifford, suicide, p. 108
behavior
    defined, p. 5
    influences on, p. 12

behavioral changes, p. 57
behavioral science, goal of, p. 1
beliefs, biases, p. 18
beneficial fear, p. 101
Bhutan, life satisfaction, pp. 44-45
bias, pp. 17-19
    appearance, pp. 17-18
    choice-supportive, p. 20
    confirmation, pp. 24, 30
    self-serving, p. 86
    reporting, p. 31
    beliefs, p. 18
bounded rationality, p. 51
brain function, p. 74
brain structures, size of, p. 59
Business Intelligence software, p. 28
buyer expectations, p. 9
Cannon, Walter, anger, p. 84
Carnegie, Dale, making friends, p. 119
Casey, B. J., judgment, p. 99
changing the brain, pp. 59-61
character defense, p. 84
child abuse intervention, prob-

lems of, pp. 71-72
child development, pp. 69-70
 encouragement, p. 66
 environment, p. 81
 learning by example, p. 66
childhood adversity, mental disorders, p. 67
choice architectures, pp. 26-27
choices, judgment, p. 21
choice-supportive bias, p. 20
chronic stress, pp. 96-97
citizen satisfaction, pp. 44-45
classical conditioning, p. 36
cognitive limitations, responsibility, p. 97
commitment, pp. 55-56
 decline of, p. 56
 escalation of, p. 56
communication skills, pp. 122-123
con-artist, p. 88
conditioning
 classical, p. 36
 defined, p. 58
 physical, pp. 73-75
 principle of, p. 58
confidence factor, relationships, p. 121
confirmation bias, pp. 24, 30
conflict resolution skills, pp. 123-125
conflict
 causes, p. 123
 handling, p. 124
conscience, defined, p. 30
consumer behavior, pp. 42-43
contract law, reason for, p. 41
corporal punishment, problems of, p. 69
Corporate Social Responsibility, p. 127
creative process pp. 48-49
creativity
 defined p. 48
 improving, p. 48

 motivation for, p. 49
criminal stigma, pp. 135-136
cronyism, p. 93
cultural value, pp. 11
decision making, software, p. 28
decisions, answering for, pp. 83-85
default options, p. 27
delaying marriage, p. 51
demand, increasing, p. 10
dependability, pp. 120-122
depression, pp. 112-114
detrimental fear, p. 101
diminishing returns, pp. 29-30
discovery process, p. 48
discovery, empirical, pp. 61-62
dissatisfaction, as motivation, p. 33
Doidge, Norman, neuroplasticity, p. 60
Duhigg, Charles
 commitment, p. 55
 habits, p. 15
 simplifying choices, pp. 27-28
Durkheim, Emile, child development, p. 65
Economics, motivation, p. 4
economics, satisfaction, pp. 42-44
effective communication, p. 122
emotional abuse, pp. 68-69
emotional branding, p. 9
emotional defense, p. 84
emotional disorders
 causes, p. 3
 development, p. 58
emotions and labeling, p. 35
emotions
 memory, p. 38
 motivation, p. 35
empirical discovery, pp. 61-62
 defined, p. 61
encouragement

agents of, pp. 65-67
child development, p. 66
ending conflict, p. 124
ending harmful relationships, pp. 125-126
Energy Balance, p. 75
environment, child development, p. 81
eustress, p. 95
excuses from responsibility, p. 86
expectancy effect, pp. 24-25
experience, learning from, p. 21
extreme devotion, p. 82
failing students, reasons for, p. 8
fair exchange, defined, p. 41
fairness
    cultural differences, pp 40-41
    defined, p. 41
fake news, p. 31
fast food diet, p. 74
favoritism, p. 93
fear localization, p. 36
fear, pp. 100-102
felony, defined, p. 133
fight-or-flight response, pp. 100, 102
fMRI, pp. 59, 99
Foss, Adam, troubled youth, p. 139
Freud, Sigmund
    delusion of persecution, p. 86
    sexual overvaluation, p. 121
Fromm, Eric, rationalization, p. 85
gains
    happiness, pp. 39-40
    influence of, pp. 39-42
    motivating productivity, p. 40
Gambler's Fallacy, p. 19

genetic influence, p. 81
Gestalt psychology, p. 48
Gilovich, Thomas, happiness, pp. 51-52
goals, p. 50
Golden Rule, p. 127
government mistakes, p. 131
government programs, public satisfaction, pp. 44-46
Gross National Happiness, pp. 44-45
habits
    defined, p. 15
    development of, p. 16
happiness
    gains, pp. 39-40
    opportunity cost, pp. 51-52
heuristics, pp. 16-17
Hotel Rwanda, pp. 37-38
Howell, Ryan, happiness, pp. 51-52
hurricane Katrina, p. 97
hypothalamus, p. 98
incentive systems, pp. 92-93
income, happiness, p. 43
information
    diminishing returns, p. 30
    quality of, pp. 23-25
informed decisions, problem of, p. 20
interpreting motivation, social skill, p. 7
intrinsic motivation, pp 7-8
intuition, problem of, p. 20
irrational tendencies, motivation, p. 6
judgment
    under stress, p. 102
    choices, p. 21
    defined, p. 14
    influences, p. 14
    limitation of, pp. 25-29
Kahneman, Daniel
    decisions, p. 19
    heuristic, p. 16

loss aversion, p. 101
    sample sizes, pp. 20-21
Katrina, hurricane, p. 97
knowledge
    retention, p. 64
    transmission of, p. 61
Koob, George, addiction, p. 115
labeling and emotions, p. 35
learned helplessness, pp. 55, 113
learned responses, formation, p. 36
learning by example, child development, p. 66
life satisfaction
    defined, p. 34
    domains, p. 34
    influences, p. 35
limbic system, p. 98
lizard brain, p. 98
loss aversion, p. 101
loss, mitigating, p. 20
losses
    influence of, pp. 39-42
    regret, p. 40
Machiavelli, Niccolo, The Prince, pp. 87-88
Maier, Steven, learned helplessness, p. 113
major stressors, p. 102
making time, p. 50
manipulation, pp. 87-88
marital infidelity, p. 12
marketing, pp. 8-10
    influence, p. 80
    motivating buyers, p. 42
Maslow, Abraham
    knowledge, p. 23
    intimate relationships, p. 121
mass-shooting
    loneliness, p. 109
    mental health, p. 111
McLellan, A. Thomas, addiction, p. 115

Mediterranean Diet, p. 74
memory, emotions, p. 38
mental condition, improving, p. 57
mental disorder
    defined, p. 109
    environmental influence, p. 79
mental disorders, pp. 109-111
    childhood adversity, p. 67
    cost of, pp. 111-112
mental health
    definition, p. 117
    mass shooter, p. 111
    problems, pp. 117-118
    understanding, p. 3
minimum wage laws, p. 130
minor stressors, p. 102
misdemeanor, defined, p. 133
moral wrongs, p. 31
motivating buyers, marketing, p. 42
motivating productivity, pp. 7-8
    gains, p. 40
motivation
    applications, p. 4
    emotions, p. 35
    intrinsic, pp 7-8
    irrational tendencies, p. 6
    Private Interest Theory of, p. 5
    theory of, p. 2
motivators, defined, p. 5
murder-suicide, p. 109
negative reinforcement, p. 70
neurogenesis, p. 74
neuroplasticity, defined, p. 60
Newton, Isaac, isolation, p. 108
non-contingent reinforcement, p. 18
non-verbal communication, p. 122
nutrition, pp. 73-74
objective feedback, p. 91

obligations, pp. 81-83
    basis of, p. 34
obsessive interests, p. 13
obstruction, pp. 88-90
open source, success of, p. 7
opportunity costs, pp. 50-52
    happiness, pp. 51-52
overconfidence, p. 19
Pager, Devah, criminal stigma, p. 136
panic disorder, p. 110
Pavlov, Ivan, classical conditioning, p. 36
PEACE, pp. 30-31
Penalty Avoidance Benefit, p. 132
perceived obligations, p. 83
persecution, delusion of, p. 86
phobias
    defined, p. 110
    development of, pp. 36-37
    problem of, p. 101
Pink, Daniel motivation, p. 7
Police and Criminal Evidence Act, pp. 30-31
policy enforcement, goal of, p. 133
policy, influences on, pp. 130-131
Political Social Responsibility, p. 128
positive stress habits, p. 103
Post Traumatic Stress Disorder, pp. 2, 58, 67, 79, 97
prefrontal cortex, p. 99
primary research, p. 25
Private Interest Theory of Motivation, p. 5
problem solving skills, pp. 22-23
producer behavior, pp. 42-43
product of choices, pp. 79-80
product of environment, p. 78
productivity, defined, p. 47
Project Aristotle, p. 121

project management, p. 28
psychosomatic disorders, p. 96
public goods and services, pp. 129-130
public policy, accountability, p. 93
public satisfaction, government programs, pp. 44-46
quality of information, pp. 23-25
    defined, p. 23
    degradation, p. 24
quality of life, defined, p. 45
Rational Choice Theory, pp. 6-7
rational decisions, defined, p. 22
rationalization, pp. 85-87
    function of, p. 85
Rayner, Rosalie, conditioning, pp. 36-37
regret, losses, p. 40
rejection therapy, p. 62
relationships
    mental health, pp. 107-109
    strengthening, p. 120
repression, p. 89
responsibility
    cognitive limitations, p. 97
    defined, pp. 76-77
    increasing, pp. 90-92
    lack of, pp. 77-80
    principle of, p. 80
    scope of, pp. 78-81
risk, p. 20
    mitigation, pp. 53-55
    aversion, pp. 52-53
    tolerance, pp. 52-53
Rosenthal, Robert expectancy effect, pp. 24-25
Ross, Dorothea, Social Learning Theory, p. 66
Ross, Sheila, Social Learning Theory, p. 66

Rwandan genocide, pp. 37-38

satire news, p. 31

satisfaction
expression of, p. 33
worker, p. 55

schizophrenia, defined, p. 114

Schloter, Carsten, suicide, p. 108

secondary research, p. 25

self-confidence, pp. 62-64
benefits of, p. 65

self-control, lack of p. 102

self-serving bias, p. 86

Seligman, Martin, learned helplessness, p. 113

sexual overvaluation, p. 121

Simmel, Georg, broken love, p. 123

Simon, Herbert, bounded rationality, p. 51

simplifying choices, pp. 27-29

Skinner, B. F.
non-contingent reinforcement, p. 18
confidence p. 62

social anxiety, p. 101

Social Learning Theory, p. 66

social problems, pp. 128-129
defined, p. 3
solutions, pp. 137-139

social responsibility, defined, p. 127

social skill, interpreting motivation, p. 7

software, decision making, p. 28

solutions to social problems, pp. 137-139

standard of living, defined, p. 45

Star Trek, p. 99

Star Wars, p. 19

state of mind, changing, p. 104

Steinberg, Laurence, judgment, p. 99

stimulus generalization, p. 37

strategy, pp. 49-50

stress
management, p. 102
response habits, pp. 102-106
biological influences, pp. 98-100
biology of, p. 96
influences of, p. 103

stressors, defined p. 95

subject matter expert, p. 28

subjective wellbeing, defined, p. 35

substance use
disorder, pp. 114-117
side effects, p. 116

suicide, reasons for, p. 108

sunk cost, defined, p. 51

Sunstein, Cass choice architectures, pp. 26-27

teamwork, strengthening, p. 121

teenage parents, p. 68

teratogens, p. 68

terrible decisions, pp. 12-13

territoriality, p. 84

Tesla, Nikola, isolation, p. 108

testing effect, p. 64

testing, significance of, p. 63

Thaler, Richard choice architectures, pp. 26-27

Thuret, Sandrine, neurogenesis, p. 74

Todorov, Alexander bias, pp. 17-18

transmission of knowledge, p. 61

trust factor, relationships, p. 121

truth, defined, p. 25

Tversky, Amos
heuristic, p. 16
loss aversion, p. 101

unnecessary risk, avoiding, p. 53

value creation, pp. 10-12

values, differences in, p. 11-12
Veenhoven, Ruut,
        life satisfaction, pp. 34-35
        quality of life p. 45
Volkow, Nora, addiction, p.
115
Watson, John, conditioning,
pp. 36-37
Wauthier, Pierre, suicide, p.
108
wealth, dissatisfaction, pp. 43-
44
wellbeing, improving, p. 62
Wine Connoisseur, p. 28
work environment, stress
reduction, p. 105
worker satisfaction, p. 55
wrongful convictions, pp. 30-
31